ENGLISH AYRES

ENGLISH AYRES

A SELECTIVELY ANNOTATED
BIBLIOGRAPHY AND DISCOGRAPHY

Compiled by Joan Swanekamp

GREENWOOD PRESS
Westport, Connecticut • London, England

Library of Congress Cataloging in Publication Data

Swanekamp, Joan.
  English ayres.

  Includes indexes.
  1. Songs, English—England—16th century—
Bibliography. 2. Songs, English—England—17th
century—Bibliography. 3. Songs, lute acc.—
Bibliography. 4. Songs, English—England—16th
century—Discography. 5. Songs, English—England—
17th century—Discography. 6. Songs, lute acc.—
Discography. I. Title.
ML128.S3S9 1984   016.7843'00942   83-18345
ISBN 0-313-23467-1 (lib. bdg.)

Library of Congress Catalog Card Number: 83-18345
ISBN: 0-313-23467-1

First published in 1984

Greenwood Press
A division of Congressional Information Service, Inc.
88 Post Road West, Westport, Connecticut 06881

Printed in the United States of America

10 9 8 7 6 5 4 3 2 1

CONTENTS

PREFACE

In 1926 Philip Heseltine, under the pseudonym of Peter Warlock, published *The English Ayre*, a slim volume with a brief two-page bibliography. Since that time articles and books focusing on the ayre composers have appeared with increasing frequency, as have editions and recordings of their works. This bibliography strives to bring these materials together as a companion volume to the Warlock book. It includes the composers mentioned by Warlock, as well as eight additional composers from E. H. Fellowes' *English School of Lutenist Song Writers* and *English Lute Songs*.

A number of sources were used to identify the materials listed. *Music Index*, *RILM Abstracts*, and major music dictionaries and encyclopedias provided the initial citations. Other sources include bibliographies and discographies, *Dissertation Abstracts International*, the *National Union Catalog*, and the published catalogs of The New York Public Library and the Boston Public Library. The OCLC data base was particularly helpful and provided the most comprehensive coverage of music and recordings. The holdings available at the Sibley Music Library of the Eastman School of Music of the University of Rochester were a most valuable resource.

This bibliography is arranged by composer and subdivided by literature, music, and recording categories. General materials are listed in the first chapter; literary works are arranged alphabetically by author. First editions of musical works are followed by facsimile editions where appropriate, then by later editions, derivative collections, and individually published works. Collections containing works by more than one composer are listed by title. Reviews have been omitted.

There are two indexes: the Author Index, which brings together all the literary materials by a given author, and the Title Index, which refers to composer, date of first edition, and page number. Library filing conventions have been followed; arrangement is word by word, and initial articles are ignored or omitted, as in the case of the Title Index.

While this bibliography aims to be comprehensive, a work of this nature is never complete. My hope is that bringing these materials together will facilitate research in this area until a definitive, up-to-date book on the English ayre appears.

ACKNOWLEDGMENTS

I wish to thank Ross Wood, Reference Librarian at the Sibley Music Library of the Eastman School of Music, Richard Smiraglia, Music Catalog Librarian at the University of Illinois at Urbana-Champaign, and Paul Kobasa, a former editor at Greenwood Press for their helpful comments and advice regarding the organization of this volume. Special thanks go to E. Ann McCollough, Music Catalog Librarian at the Sibley Music Library of the Eastman School of Music for proofreading and typing the final copy of the bibliography. Lastly, I am thankful to the Sibley Music Library of the Eastman School of Music of the University of Rochester and all its wonderful resources.

ACKNOWLEDGMENTS

ABBREVIATIONS

accomp.	accompanied, accompaniment
Am Rec	*American Recorder*
arr.	arrange(d)
AST	*American String Teacher*
BAMS	*Bulletin of the American Musicological Society*
CNRS	Centre National de la Recherche Scientifique
Current Mus	*Current Musicology*
Diss. Abst.	*Dissertation Abstracts*
ed.	edited, editor
ELS	*English Lutesongs*, ed. by E.H. Fellowes, rev. by Thurston Dart, 1959-
EM	*Early Music*
ESLS	*English School of Lutenist Song Writers*, ed. by E.H. Fellowes, 1925-32
Galpin SJ	*Galpin Society Journal*
GR	*Guitar Review*
JAMS	*Journal of the American Musicological Society*
JLSA	*Journal of the Lute Society of America*
LSJ	*Lute Society Journal (London)*
MA	*Musical Antiquary*
M&L	*Music and Letters*
MD	*Musica Disciplina*
Mens en Mel	*Mens en Melodie*
MfM	*Monatshefte für Musikgeschichte*
MGG	*Musik in Geschichte und Gegenwart*
MLQ	*Modern Language Quarterly*
MM	*Miscellanea Musicologica*

MMR	*Monthly Musical Record*
MusR	*Music Review*
MT	*Musical Times*
Mus & Mus	*Music and Musicians*
Mus Events	*Musical Events*
Mus Survey	*Music Survey*
New Grove	*The New Grove Dictionary of Music and Musicians*
NOHM	*New Oxford History of Music*
OUP	Oxford University Press
PMA	*Proceedings of the Musical Association*
PMLA	*Publications of the Modern Language Associaton of America*
PRMA	*Proceedings of the Royal Musical Association*
RenaisN	*Renaissance News*
RMA	Royal Musical Association
RMA Research	*Royal Musical Association Research Chronicle*
RMM	*Record and Music Magazine*
SIMG	*Sammelbande der Internationalen Musikgesellschaft*
Studies Mus	*Studies in Music*
trans.	transcribe(d)
unpubl.	unpublished

ENGLISH AYRES

AYRE

General literature

1. Anderton, H. Orsmond. Early English music. London: Musical Opinion, 1920. 344 p.

2. Apel, Willi.· The notation of polyphonic music, 900-1600. Cambridge, Mass.: Medieval Academy of America, 1942; rev. ed. 1944, 1949.

   New ed. published as: Die Notation der polyphonen Musik, 900-1600. Leipzig: Breitkopf u. Härtel, 1962; 2. verb. Aufl., 1970.

3. Arkwright, G. E. P. Catalogue of music in the library of Christ Church, Oxford. London: OUP, 1915-1923. 2 v.

4. Auden, William H. An Elizabethan song book. London: Faber and Faber, 1957. 240 p.

5. Ault, Norman. Elizabethan lyrics from the original texts. London: Longmans, 1925. 535 p.

   2d ed.: London; New York: Longmans, 1928. 536 p.
   3d ed.: New York: W. Sloane, 1949. 560 p.

6. Bernstein, Jane. The chanson in England, 1530-1640: a study of sources and styles. Unpubl. Ph.D. diss., University of California, Berkeley, 1974.

7. Bontoux, Germaine. La chanson en Angleterre au temps d'Elizabeth. Oxford: OUP, 1936. 699 p.

   Literary and musical origins are examined and the foreign influence on secular song is discussed. Includes musical examples.

8.   Boyd, Morrison C. _Elizabethan music and music criticism_.
Philadelphia, Penn.: University of Pennsylvania Press, 1940. 363 p.

> 2d ed.: 1962.
> A survey of literature on Elizabethan music.

9.   Brett, Philip. "The English consort song, 1570-1625." _PRMA_
LXXXVIII (1961/62):73-88.

10. Brown, Howard. _Music in the Renaissance_. Englewood Cliffs:
Prentice-Hall, 1976. 384 p.

11. Browne, James. "An Elizabethan song-cycle." _The Cornhill Magazine_
XLVIII (1920):572-79.

12. Bukofzer, Manfred F. "The first English chanson on the Continent."
_M&L_ XIX (1938):119-31.

13. Burney, Charles. _A general history of music, from the earliest
ages to the present period_. London: Printed for the author, 1776-1789.
4 v.

> Reprint ed. New York: Harcourt, Brace & Co., 1935. 2 v.
> Reprint ed. New York: Dover, 1957. 2 v.

14. Buxton, John. _Elizabethan taste_. New York: Macmillan, 1963, 1965.
370 p.

> Survey of aesthetic sentiment. Music included p. 171-220.

15. Byler, A. W. _Italian currents in the popular music of England in
the sixteenth century_. Unpubl. diss. (Ph.D.), University of Chicago,
1952.

16. Carpenter, Nan Cooke. "The study of music at the University of
Oxford in the Renaissance (1450-1600)." _MQ_ XLI (1955):191-214.

> Extracted from: _Music in the Medieval and Renaissance universities_.
> Norman, Okla.: University Press, 1958. 394 p.

17. Casey, W. S. "Dissertations: Printed English lute instruction
books, 1568-1610. Reviewed by J. Sutton." _Current Mus_ (Fall 1965):
202-207.

18. Chambers, E. K. and F. Sidgwick. _Early English lyrics_. London:
Sidgwick & Jackson, 1921. 384 p.

19. Chambers, E. K. _The Elizabethan stage_. Oxford: Clarendon, 1923.
4 v.

> Reprint ed.: 1967.

20. Chappell, William. _The ballad literature and popular music of olden
time_. London: Chappell, 1855-1859? 2 v.

> New York: Dover, 1965. new introduction.

21. Colles, H. C. and Robert Donington. "Air." Grove's dictionary of music and musicians, 5th ed. New York: St. Martin's Press, 1954. I:78.

Short discussion of the ayre and related forms; includes bibliography.

22. Cutts, John P. "A Bodleian song book: Don. C. 57." M&L XXXIV (1953):192ff.

23. Cutts, John P. "Drexel manuscript 4041." MD XVIII (1964):151ff.

24. Cutts, John P. "Early seventeenth-century lyrics at St. Michaels College, Tenbury." M&L XXXVII (1956):221-33.

25. Cutts, John P. "Mris Elizabeth Davenant 1624: Christ Church MS Mus. 87." Review of English Studies, new ser. X (1959):26ff.

26. Cutts, John P. La musique de scène de la troupe de Shakespeare. Paris: CNRS, 1959. 198 p.

2d ed.: Paris: CNRS, 1971.

27. Cutts, John P. "Le rôle de la musique dans les masques de Ben Jonson, et notamment dans Oberon (1610-1611)." In: Jacquot. Fetes de la Renaissance I. 1956. p. 285-303.

Pieces by Robert Johnson and Ferrabosco: p. 294-300.

28. Cutts, John P. "Seventeenth-century lyrics: Oxford, Bodleian, MS. Mus. Sch.b.I." MD X (1956):142-209.

Lists contents of manuscript.

29. Cutts, John P. "Seventeenth-century songs and lyrics in Edinburgh University Library, Music MS. Dc.I.69." MD XIII (1959):169-94.

Includes an annotated list of the contents.

30. Cutts, John P. "Songs unto violl and lute: Drexel MS. 4175." MD XVI (1962):73-90.

The contents (p. 78-79) is compared with BM add. MS. 29481.

31. Cyr, Mary. "Song accompaniment for the lyra viol and lute." JLSA IV (1971):43-49.

32. Dart, Thurston. "Rôle de la danse dans l'ayre anglais." In: Musique et poésie au XVIe siecle. Paris: CNRS, 1954. p. 203-209.

Relates English ayre to continental styles.

33. Davey, Henry. History of English music. London: J. Curwen, 1895. 518 p.

2d ed.: London: J. Curwen, 1921. 505 p.
2d ed. reprinted: New York: Da Capo, 1969. 505 p.
Discusses manuscript sources.

34. De Lafontaine, Henry Cart. The King's musick. London: Novello, 1909. 522 p.

    Reprint ed.: New York: Da Capo Press, 1973.
    "... a transcript of records relating to music and musicians (1460-1700)."

35. Deakin, Andrew. Outlines of musical bibliography: a catalogue of early and musical works printed or otherwise produced in the British Isles. The whole chronologically arranged, with descriptive and critical notes on the principal works. Birmingham: Deakin, 1899. Part I only published - To 1650.

    Originally planned to stop at 1800. Chronological list of music literature and music, manuscript and printed, as well as drama and works on drama. Author index, and index of title of manuscript and anonymous works.

36. Delattre, Floris and Camille Chemin. Les chansons élizabéthaines. Paris: Didier, 1948. 459 p.

    From the series: Bibliothèque des langues modernes, II. Includes bibliography; introduction and p. 34-63 deal with Elizabethan music.

37. Dodge, Janet. "Lutenists and lute music in England." Euterpe VII (1970):34ff.

38. Dolmetsch, Arnold. The interpretation of the music of the 17th and 18th centuries. London: Novello; New York: H.W. Gray, 1915. 433 p.

    New ed.: London: Novello, 1946. 493 p.
    Includes music.

39. Donington, Robert. "The English contribution to the growth of chamber music." Mus Survey IV (1951):341.

40. Doughtie, Edward. Lyrics from English airs, 1596-1622. Cambridge, Mass.: Harvard University Press, 1970. 657 p.

    An important study which reproduces the texts and sets forth information concerning the date and authorship of each poem. Variant forms are discussed as well as including incidental information.

41. Doughtie, Edward. "Words and music: simplicity and complexity in the Elizabethan ayre." Rice University Studies LI (1965):1.

42. Duckles, Vincent. "The English musical elegy of the late Renaissance." In: La Rue, ed. Aspects of medieval and Renaissance music. New York, 1966. p. 134-53.

    Includes list of elegies, sources and modern editions.

43. Duckles, Vincent. "Florid embellishments in English song of the late sixteenth and early seventeenth centuries." AnnM V (1957):329-45.

Fifty florid songs are listed with composers, authors and sources.

44. Duckles, Vincent. "The Gamble Manuscript as a source of continuo song in England." JAMS I (Summer 1948):23-40.

45. Edwards, Warwick. "The performance of ensemble music in Elizabethan England." PRMA XCVII (1970/71):113-23.

46. Eitner, Robert. Biographisch-Bibliographisches Quellen-Lexikon der Musiker und Musikgelehrten. Leipzig: Breitkopf & Härtel, 1900-1904. 10 v.

47. Emslie, MacDonald. The relationship between words and music in English secular song, 1622-1700. Ph.D. Diss., Cambridge University, 1958.

48. Evans, Herbert Arthur. English masques. London: Blackie & Son; New York: Charles Scribner's Sons, 1897. 245 p.

49. Evans, Willa McClung. Ben Jonson and Elizabethan music. Lancaster, Pa.: Lancaster Press, 1929. 131 p.

Reprint ed.: New York: Da Capo Press, 1965.

50. Fellowes, Edmund H. The catalogue of manuscripts in the library of St. Michael's College, Tenbury. Paris: Oiseau-Lyre, 1934. 319 p.

51. Fellowes, Edmund H. "The English lutenists." Sackbut II (1922): 36ff.

52. Fellowes, Edmund H. The English madrigal. Oxford: OUP, 1925. 111 p.

53. Fellowes, Edmund H. The English madrigal composers. Oxford: OUP, 1921. 364 p.

2d ed.: 1948.
Includes lute songs. Part I: General survey. Part II: The composers and their music. Also includes index to first lines, list of surviving copies of first editions, and biographical table.

54. Fellowes, Edmund H. English madrigal verse, 1588-1632. Oxford: Clarendon Press, 1920. 640 p.

2d ed.: Oxford: Clarendon Press, 1929. 644 p.
3d ed.: Oxford: Clarendon Press, 1967. 798 p.
Reproduces texts for madrigals and lute songs.

55. Finney, Gretchen Ludke. Musical backgrounds for English literature: 1580-1650. New Brunswick, NJ: Rutgers University Press, 1962. 292 p.

Reprint ed.: Westport, Conn.: Greenwood Press, 1976.

56. Ford, Wyn K. Music in England before 1800: a select bibliography. London: The Library Association, 1967. 128 p.

57. Fortune, Nigel. "Solo song and cantata." NOHM IV (1968):191-94.

58. Fuller, David. "The Jonsonian masque and its music." M&L LIV (1973):440-52.

59. Gladding, Bessie A. "Music as a social force during the English Commonwealth and Restoration." MQ XV (1929):506-21.

60. Greer, David. "The part-songs of the English lutenists." PRMA XCIV (1967/68):97-110.

61. Greer, David. "Songbooks 1500-1660." New Cambridge bibliography of English literature. Cambridge, Eng.: Cambridge University Press, 1969-77. 5 v.

62. Hall, James Husst. The art song. Norman, Okla.: University of Oklahoma Press, 1953. 310 p.

    The discussion includes a chapter devoted to the "Elizabethans and their successors." Includes bibliography.

63. Hall, Hubert. Society in the Elizabethan age. London: Sonnenschein, 1886.

64. Hawkins, Sir John. A general history of the science and practice of music. London: Printed for T. Payne. 1776. 5 v.

    Reprint ed.: New York: Dover, 1963. 2 v.

65. Hollander, John. The untuning of the sky; ideas of music in English poetry, 1500-1700. Princeton: Princeton University Press, 1961. 467 p.

    Survey of the treatment of music in poetry. Bibliography covers primary and secondary sources.
    New ed.: New York: W.W. Norton, 1970.

66. Hooton, M. "Music and dance in Elizabethan life." American Recorder XV (1974):118-26.

67. Hough, John. "The historical significance of the counter-tenor." PRMA LXIV (1938):1-24.

68. Hughes-Hughes, Augustus. Catalogue of manuscript music in the British Museum. London: Trustees of the British Museum, 1906-1909. 3 v.

    Photolithographic reprint of v. 1, 1964.

69.. Ing, Catherine. Elizabethan lyrics. London: Chatto & Windus, 1951. 252 p.

A study in the development of English meters and their relation
to poetic effect. Includes bibliography.
Chapters devoted to Elizabethan lyrics influenced by music and
Thomas Campion.

70. Ingram, R. W. Dramatic use of music in English drama, 1603-1642.
Ph.D. diss., London, 1955.

71. Johnson, Paula. Form and transformation in music and poetry of
the English Renaissance. New Haven; London: Yale University Press,
1972. 170 p.

Extensive bibliography and discography.

72. Joiner, Mary. "British Museum Add. Ms. 15117: a commentary,
index and bibliography." RMA Research VII (1967):51-109.

73. Jones, E. H. "'To sing and play the base-violl alone': the bass
viol in English 17th century song." LSJ XVII (1975):17.

74. Jorgens, Elsie Bickford. "Let well-tun'd words amaze"--attitudes
toward poetry in English solo song from John Dowland to Henry Lawes.
Ph.D. diss., City University of New York, 1975. Diss. Abst. XXXVI
(Oct. 1975):1890A.

75. Jorgens, Elsie Bickford. The well-tun'd word; musical interpretations of English poetry, 1597-1651. Minneapolis: University of
Minnesota Press, 1982. 298 p.

Includes many musical examples and bibliography.

76. Kelso, Ruth. The doctrine of the English gentleman in the
sixteenth century. With a bibliographical list of treatises on the
gentleman and related subjects published in Europe to 1625. Urbana:
University of Illinois Press, 1929. 288 p.

77. Kerman, Joseph. The Elizabethan madrigal: a comparative study.
Philadelphia: American Musicological Society, 1962. 318 p.

78. Kidson, Frank. British music publishers, printers and engravers
... from Queen Elizabeth's reign to George the Fourth. With select
bibliographical lists of musical works printed and published within
that period. London: Hill, 1900. 231 p.

Reprint ed.: New York: B. Blom, 1967.
Arranged by location; lists work published.

79. Lawrence, W. J. "Music in the Elizabethan theatre." MQ VI
(1920):192-205.

80. Le Huray, P. Music and the Reformation in England, 1549-1660.
London; New York: OUP, 1967. 454 p.

Reprinted with corrections, 1978.

81. Long, John H. Music in English Renaissance drama. Lexington: University of Kentucky Press, 1968. 184 p.

82. Long, John H. Shakespeare's use of song. Gainesville, Florida: University of Florida Press, 1955. 213 p.

Reprint ed.: Da Capo Press, 1977.

83. Lowe, M. "The historical development of the lute in the 17th century." Galpin SJ XXIX (1976):14.

84. Lumsden, David. "English lute music 1540-1620, an introduction." PRMA LXXXIII (1956/57):1-13.

85. Lumsden, David. "The lute in England." The Score VIII (Sept. 1953):36-43.

86. Lumsden, David. The sources of English lute music, 1540-1620. Unpubl. Ph.D. diss., Cambridge (Eng.), 1955. 3 v.

87. Lumsden, David. "The sources of English lute music (1540-1620)." Galpin SJ VI (1953):14-22.

88. La luth et sa musique. Paris: CNRS, 1958. 356 p.

2d ed.: 1976.

89. Mackerness, Eric David. A social history of English music. London: Routledge and Kegan Paul; Toronto: University of Toronto Press, 1964, with corrections in 1966. 307 p.

90. Manifold, John S. The music in English drama from Shakespeare to Purcell. London: Rockliff, 1956. 208 p.

91. Manifold, John S. "Theatre music in the sixteenth and seventeenth centuries." M&L (1948):366-397.

92. Mark, Jeffrey. "The Jonsonian masque." M&L III (1922):358-71.

93. Mark, Jeffrey. "The song cycle in England: some early 17th century examples." MT LXVI (1925):325-28.

94. McGrady, Richard J. The English solo song from William Byrd to Henry Lawes; a study of the relationships between poetry and music during the period c. 1588-1622. Ph.D. diss., University of Manchester, 1963.

95. McGrady, Richard J. "Henry Lawes and the concept of 'just note and accent.'" M&L L (1969):86-102.

96. Mellers, Wilfred H. Harmonious meeting. London: D. Dobson, 1965. 317 p.

A study in the relationship between English poetry, music and theatre, 1600-1900.

97.   Mellers, Wilfred H.   "Words and music in Elizabethan England."
In: The age of Shakespeare, edited by Boris Ford. Harmondsworth:
Pelican Guides to English Literature, 2, 1955.

98.   Monson, Craig. Voices and viols in England, 1600-1650; the
sources and the music. Ann Arbor: UMI Research Press, 1982. 360 p.

    A revision of the author's thesis: University of California,
    Berkeley, 1974.
    Includes index.

99.   Morris, Reginald Owen. "Some technical features of the English
School." In: Contrapuntal techniques in the sixteenth century.
Oxford: Clarendon Press, 1922. p. 64-74.

100. Nagel, Willibald. Annalen der englischen Hofmusik, 1509-1649.
Leipzig: Breitkopf & Härtel, 1894. 82 p.

101. Naylor, Edward W. "Music and Shakespeare." MA I (1910):129-148.

102. Naylor, Edward W. Shakespeare and music. London: Dent, 1896.
225 p.

    Rev. ed.: London: Dent; New York: Dutton, 1931. 212 p.
    Reprint ed.: New York: Da Capo Press, 1965.

103. Newcomb, Wilburn W. Studien zur englischen Lautenpraxis im
elisabethanischen Zeitalter. Kassel: Barenreiter, 1968. 135 p.

104. Newton, Richard. "English lute music of the Golden Age."
PRMA LXV (1939):63-90.

105. Nicoll, Allardyce. Stuart masques and the Renaissance stage.
New York: Harcourt, Brace & Co., 1938. 223 p.

    Reprint ed.: New York: Arno, 1980.

106. Noble, Richmond S. H. Shakespeare's use of song. London: OUP,
1923. 160 p.

    Reprint ed.: Oxford: Clarendon, 1966.

107. Northcote, Sydney. Byrd to Britten: a survey of English song.
London: John Baker, 1966. 152 p.

108. Nye, Nancy L. The songs of the English lutenists. Master's
thesis, Texas Christian University, 1950. 152 p.

109. Oboussier, Philippe. "Turpyn's book of lute songs." M&L
XXXIV (1958):145-49.

    Gives contents of the MS. in the Rowe Music Library, King's
    College, Cambridge.

110. Olshausen, Ulrich. Das lautenbegleitete Solo-Lied in England um
1600. Ph.D. diss. published Kassel: Barenreiter, 1963. 342 p.

111. Pattison, Bruce. "Literature and music in the age of Shakespeare."
PRMA LX (1934):67-86.

112. Pattison, Bruce. Music and poetry of the English Renaissance.
London: Methuen & Co., Ltd., 1948. 222 p.

> 2d ed.: 1970.
> Chapter 7 is devoted to the ayre (air) and mentions the following
> composers: Barley, Bartlet, Campion, Cavendish, Cooper (Coprario),
> Corkine, Daniel (Danyel), Dowland, Ferrabosco, Hume, Jones,
> Morley, Pilkington and Rosseter.

113. Pattison, Bruce. "A note on the 16th century lute songs."
MT LXXI (1930):796-98.

114. Peacham, Henry. The compleat gentleman. 1622. In: Strunk,
Oliver, comp. Source readings in music history: from classical
antiquity through the romantic era. New York: Norton, 1950. p. 331-37.

115. Pearson, A. B. English song from John Dowland to John Blow.
B. Litt., Oxford, 1956.

116. Poulton, Diana and David Mitchell. "List of printed lute music
in the British Museum."

> Part I - LSJ XIII (1971):40-49.
> Part II - LSJ XIV (1972):42-50.

117. Price, Shelby M. The restoration verse anthem. Ph.D. diss.,
University of Southern California, 1967. Diss. Abst. XXVIII (Feb.
1968):3213A.

118. Pulver, Jeffrey. A biographical dictionary of old English music.
London: K. Paul, Trench, Trubner; New York: E. P. Dutton, 1927. 537 p.

> Reprint ed.: New York: B. Franklin, 1969.
> Reprint ed.: New York: Da Capo, 1973.

119. Pulver, Jeffrey. A dictionary of old English music & musical
instruments. London: K. Paul, Trench, Trubner; New York: E. P. Dutton,
1923. 247 p.

120. Puttenham, George and Richard Puttenham. The arte of English
poesie. London: Harding and Wright for R. Triphook, 1811. 258 p.

> Reprint ed.: Cambridge: Cambridge University Press, 1936.
> Reprint ed.: Norwood, Pa.: Norwood Editions, 1978.

121. Raynor, Henry. "Framed to the life of words." MusR XIX (1958):
261-72.

122. Reese, Gustave. Music in the Renaissance. New York: Norton,
1954. 1022 p.

> Rev. ed.: 1959.

123. Reyher, Paul. Les masques anglais: étude sur les ballets et la vie de cour in Angleterre. Paris: Hachette, 1909. 563 p.

> Reprint ed.: New York: B. Błom, 1964.
> List of entertainments, 1603-40 (p. 519-32). Music is discussed in Chapter VII and Appendix III. Includes bibliography.

124. Rowse, A. L. The England of Elizabeth: the structure of society. New York: Macmillan, 1950. 547 p.

125. Ruff, Lillian M. and D. Arnold Wilson. "Allusion to the Essex downfall in lute song lyrics." LSJ XII (1970):31-36.

126. Ruff, Lillian M. and D. Arnold Wilson. "The lute song and Elizabethan politics." Past and Present XLIV (1969):3-51.

127. Sabol, Andrew J. Songs and dances for the Stuart masque. Providence, R.I.: Brown University Press, 1959. 172 p.

> "An edition of 63 items of music for the English court masque from 1604 to 1641, with introductory essay."
> 1978 ed.: Four hundred songs and dances for the Stuart masque.

128. Schnapper, Edith. British union catalogue of early music printed before the year 1800. A record of the holdings of over one hundred libraries throughout the British Isles. London: Butterworth, 1957. 2 v.

129. Scholl, Evely H. A study of the English school of lutenist song-writers. Unpubl. Ph.D. diss., University of Michigan, Ann Arbor, 1935.

130. Scott, M. A. Elizabethan translations from the Italian. Boston: Houghton Mifflin, 1916. 558 p.

131. Smith, James G. John Dowland: a reappraisal of his ayres. Unpubl. D.M.A. thesis, University of Illinois, Urbana, 1973. 457 p. Diss. Abst. XXXIV (March 1974):6030A.

132. Smith, Leo. Music of the seventeenth and eighteenth centuries. London: J. M. Dent, 1931. 280 p.

133. Spink, Ian. "English cavalier songs, 1620-1660." PRMA LXXXVI (1959):61-78.

134. Spink, Ian. The English declamatory ayre from c. 1620-1660. M.A. thesis, University of Birmingham (Eng.), 1958.

135. Spink, Ian. English song: Dowland to Purcell. New York: Charles Scribner's Sons, 1974. 312 p.

> London: B. T. Batsford, 1974.

136. Spink, Ian. "Sources of English song 1620-1660: a survey." MM I (1966):117-36.

137. Steele, Mary Susan. <u>Plays and masques at court during the reigns of Elizabeth, James and Charles</u>. New Haven: Yale University Press, 1926. 300 p.

List of masques by Campion and Ford. Index arranged by author and title.

138. Sullivan, Mary. <u>Court masques of James I; their influence on Shakespeare and the public theatres</u>. New York; London: G. P. Putnam's Sons, 1913. 259 p.

139. Tegnell, John C. <u>Elizabethan prosody: a study of the style of the English madrigal and ayre</u>. Unpubl. Ph.D. diss., Northwestern University, 1949. 248 p.

140. Walker, Ernest. <u>A history of music in England</u>. Oxford: Clarendon Press, 1907. 364 p.

2d ed.: London: OUP, 1924. 386 p.
3d ed.: London: Clarendon Press, 1952. 468 p. Revised by J. A. Westrup with footnotes and bibliography arranged by chapter.

141. Ward, John. "Music for a handfull of pleasant delites." <u>JAMS</u> X (1957):151-80.

142. Warlock, Peter. <u>The English ayre</u>. London: OUP, 1926. 142 p.

Reprint ed.: Westwood, Conn.: Greenwood Press, 1970.
This slim volume is THE book on the English ayre; chapters devoted to Dowland, Danyel, Jones, Hume, Ferrabosco, Campion and Rosseter. Also covers Cavendish, Greaves, Corkine, Ford, Pilkington, Morley, Bartlet, Cooper, Maynard, Peerson and Attey. Includes a chronological table.

143. Warlock, Peter. <u>English ayres, Elizabethan and Jacobean: a discourse</u>. Oxford: OUP, 1932. 32 p.

Intended as a forward to an edition of the music.

144. Weslford, Enid. <u>The court masque: a study of the relationship between poetry & the revels</u>. Cambridge: Cambridge University Press, 1927. 434 p.

Reprint ed.: New York: Russell & Russell, 1962.

145. Westrup, Jack A. "Domestic music under the Stuarts." <u>PRMA</u> LXVIII (1942):19-53.

146. Wilson, John. <u>Roger North on music</u>. London: Novello, 1959. 372 p.

"... Being a selection from his essays written during the years c. 1695-1728."

147. Woodfill, Walter L. <u>Musicians in English society. From Elizabeth to Charles I</u>. Princeton: Princeton University Press, 1953. 372 p.

Extensive bibliography; includes MSS. and primary and
secondary sources.
Reprint ed.: New York: Da Capo Press, 1969.

148. Wright, Louis. Middle-class culture in Elizabethan England.
Chapel Hill, NC: University of North Carolina Press, 1935. 733 p.

Reprint ed.: Octagon Press, 1980.

149. Zimmerman, Franklin B. "Air: a catchword for new concepts in
seventeenth-century English music theory." Studies in musicology in
honor of Otto E. Albrecht. Kassel: Barenreiter, 1977. 287 p.

150. Zimmermann, Franklin B. Features of Italian style in Elizabethan
part-songs and madrigals: a comparative study of the works of Marenzio,
Ferrabosco, Byrd, Morley and Weelkes. B. Litt., Oxford, 1956.

Music

151. English ayres, Elizabethan and Jacobean. Transcribed and edited
from the original editions by Peter Warlock (Philip Heseltine) and
Philip Wilson. London: OUP, 1927-31. 6 v.

152. The English school of lutenist song writers. Trans., scored and
ed. from the original ed. by Edmund Horace Fellowes. Series 1. London:
Winthrop Rogers; New York: G. Schirmer, 1920-32. 16 v.

V. 2, 12-16 have imprint: London: Stainer & Bell.
For solo voice; the original accomp. is printed both in lute
tablature and in modern notation; an alternative version
especially adapted for piano is also given with each song.

Contents:
v.1-2   Dowland, John. First book of airs. 1597.
v.3   Ford, Thomas. Airs for the lute from Musicke of
          sundrie kindes. 1607.
v.4,13   Campion, Thomas. Songs from Rosseter's Book of airs.
          1601.
v.5-6   Dowland, John. Second book of airs. 1600.
v.7,15   Pilkington, Francis. First book of songs or airs. 1605.
v.8-9   Rosseter, Philip. Songs from Rosseter's Book of airs.
          1601.
v.10-11   Dowland, John. Third book of airs. 1603.
v.12,14   Dowland, John. A pilgrimes solace (Fourth book of airs).
          1612. Three songs included in a "Musicall banquet."
          1610.
v.16   Morley, Thomas. First book of airs. 1600.

Revised and continued by: The English lute-songs. Ser. 1.

153. The English school of lutenist song writers. Ser. 2. Trans.,
scored and ed. from the original ed. by Edmund Horace Fellowes.
London: Stainer & Bell, 1925-27. 16 v.

For 1 or 2 voices; original accomp. trans. into modern notation
for the piano.
Revised and continued by: The English lute-songs. Ser. 2.

Contents:
v.1   Campion, Thomas. First book of airs. ca. 1613.
v.2   Campion, Thomas. Second book of airs. ca. 1613.
v.3   Bartlet, John. A booke of ayres. 1606.
v.4   Jones, Robert. First booke of songs and ayres. 1600.
v.5   Jones, Robert. Second booke of ayres. 1601.
v.6   Jones, Robert. Ultimum vale, third booke of ayres. 1608.
v.7   Cavendish, Michael. Songs included in Michael Cavendish's
       Booke of ayres and madrigalles. 1598.
v.8   Daniel, John. Songs for the lute, viol and voice. 1606.
v.9   Attey, John. First booke of ayres. 1622.
v.10   Campion, Thomas. Third booke of ayres. ca. 1617.
v.11   Campion, Thomas. Fourth booke of ayres. ca. 1617.
v.12   Corkine, William. First booke of ayres. 1610.
v.13   Corkine, William. Second booke of ayres. 1612.
v.14   Jones, Robert. A musicall dreame: or, Fourth booke of
       ayres. 1609.
v.15   Jones, Robert. The muses gardin for delights; or, Fifth
       booke of ayres. 1610.
v.16   Ferrabosco, Alfonso. Ayres. 1609.

154. The English lute-songs. Ser. 1. Revised by Thurston Dart.
London: Stainer & Bell, 1959-   v. 1-

Revises and continues: The English school of lutenist song
writers. Ser. 1.

Contents:
v.1-16 SEE English school of lutenist song writers. Ser. 1.
v.17   Coperario, John. Funeral teares (1606). Songs of
        mourning (1613). The masque of squires (1614).

155. The English lute-songs. Ser. 2. Revised by Thurston Dart.
London: Stainer & Bell, 1959-   v. 1-

Revises and continues: The English school of lutenist song
writers. Ser. 2.

Contents:
v.1-16 SEE English school of lutenist song writers. Ser. 2.
v.17   Johnson, Robert. Ayres, songs, and dialogues.
v.18   Greaves, Thomas. Songs of sundrie kindes. 1604.
        George Mason's and John Earsden's ayres. 1618.
v.19   Ferrabosco, Alfonso, Manuscript songs.
v.20   Dowland, Robert. A musicall banquet. 1610.
v.21   Twenty songs from printed sources.

156. English lute songs, 1597-1632: a collection of facsimile reprints.
General editor: F.W. Sternfeld. Menston, Eng.: Scolar Press,
1968-1971. 36 v.

Contents:
v.1 Alison, Richard. The psalmes of David in meter. 1599.
v.2 Attey, John. The first booke of ayres. 1622.
v.3 Bartlet, John. A booke of ayres. 1606.
v.4 Campion, Thomas. Two bookes of ayres. ca. 1613.
v.5 Campion, Thomas. The third and fourth booke of ayres.
     ca. 1618.
v.6 Campion, Thomas. The description of a maske in honour of
     the Lord Hayes. 1607.
v.7 Campion, Thomas. The description of a maske presented at
     the mariage of the Earle of Somerset. 1614.
v.8 Cavendish, Michael. 14 ayres in tabletorie to the lute.
     1598.
v.9 Coprario, John. Funeral tears. 1606.
v.10 Coprario, John. Songs of mourning. 1613.
v.11 Corkine, William. Ayres to sing and play to the lute. 1610.
v.12 Corkine, William. The second booke of ayres. 1612.
v.13 Danyel, John. Songs for the lute, viol and voice. 1606.
v.14 Dowland, John. The first booke of songes or ayres. 1597.
v.15 Dowland, John. The first booke of songs. 1613.
v.16 Dowland, John. The second booke of songs or ayres. 1600.
v.17 Dowland, John. The third and last booke of songs or ayres.
     1603.
v.18 Dowland, John. A pilgrime's solace. 1612.
v.19 Dowland, Robert. A musicall banquet. 1610.
v.20 Ferrabosco, Alfonso. Ayres. 1609.
v.21 Ford, Thomas. Musicke of sundrie kindes. 1607.
v.22 Greaves, Thomas. Songs of sundrie kindes. 1604.
v.23 Handford, George. Ayres to be sunge to the lute. ca. 1609.
v.24 Hume, Tobias. The first part of ayres. 1605.
v.25 Hume, Tobias. Poeticall musicke. 1607.
v.26 Jones, Robert. The first booke of songes or ayres. 1600.
v.27 Jones, Robert. The second booke of songs and ayres. 1601.
v.28 Jones, Robert. Ultimum vale. 1605.
v.29 Jones, Robert. A musicall dreame. 1609.
v.30 Jones, Robert. The muses' gardin. 1610.
v.31 Mason, George and John Earsden. The ayres that were sung
     and played at Brougham Castle. 1618.
v.32 Maynard, John. The XII wonders of the world. 1611.
v.33 Morley, Thomas. The first booke of ayres. 1600.
v.34 Pilkington, Francis. The first booke of songs or ayres.
     1606.
v.35 Porter, Walter. Madrigals and ayres. 1632.
v.36 Rosseter, Philip. A booke of ayres, set forth to be sung
     to the lute, orpherian and base viol. 1601.

157. Forty Elizabethan songs. Edited and arranged with the original
accompaniments by Edmund Horace Fellowes. London: Stainer & Bell,
1921. 4 v.

RICHARD ALISON
(ALLISON)

Literature

158. Anderson, Ronald E. Richard Allison's Psalter (1599) and devotational music in England to 1640. Unpubl. Ph.D. diss., University of Iowa, 1975. 724 p. Diss. Abst. XXXV (Oct. 1974):2314A-15A

159. Frost, Maurice. English & Scottish psalm & hymn tunes. London: OUP, 1953. 531 p.

160. Greer, David. "'What if a day'--an examination of the words and music." M&L XLIII (1962):304-19.

161. Poulton, Diana. "Alison, Richard." The New Grove ... London: Macmillan, 1980. I:259-60.

   Short biography with list of works and bibliography.

162. Rimbault, Edward F. "Alison, Richard." Grove's dictionary of music and musicians, 5th ed. New York: St. Martin's Press, 1954. I:110-11.

   Short biography and list of works.

Music

163. Alison, Richard. The psalmes of David in meter, the plaine song, being the common tunne to be sung and plaide ... the singing part to be either tenor or treble to the instrument ... or for foure voyces. London: William Barley, the assigne of Thomas Morley, 1599.

   RISM A/I/1 A852.
   Contents: Veni creator -- The humble sute of a sinner -- Venite exultemus -- Te deum -- The song of the three children --

Magnificat -- Nunc dimittis -- Quicunque vult -- The lamentation
-- The Lord's prayer -- The X. commandements -- The complaint of
a sinner -- Psalme 1 -- Psalme 3 -- Psalme 6 -- Psalme 14 --
Psalme 18 -- Psalme 21 -- Psalme 22 -- Psalme 25 -- Psalme 30 --
Psalme 41 -- Psalme 44 -- Psalme 46 -- Psalme 50 -- Psalme 51 --
Psalme 52 -- Psalme 59 -- Psalme 61 -- Psalme 68 -- Psalme 69 --
Psalme 72 -- Psalme 81 -- Psalme 78 -- Psalme 103 -- Psalme 104 --
Psalme 111 -- Psalme 113 -- Psalme 119 -- Psalme 121 -- Psalme
122 -- Psalme 124 -- Psalme 125 -- Psalme 126 -- Psalme 130 --
Psalme 132 -- Psalme 135 -- Psalme 136 -- Psalme 137 -- Psalme
141 -- Psalme 145 -- Psalme 147 -- Psalme 148 -- Audi Israel --
The Lord's prayer (2d version) -- The creede -- Da pacem --
The lamentation (2d version) -- A prayer -- Psalme 12 -- Psalme
50 (2d version) -- Psalme 88 -- Psalme 116.

164. Alison, Richard. The psalmes of David in meter ... 1599.
Menston, Eng.: Scolar Press, 1968. 1 v.

Facsimile of British Museum copy.
Series: English lute songs, v. 1.
Contents: SEE 163.

165. Twenty songs from printed sources. Trans. and ed. by David
Greer. London: Stainer and Bell, 1969.

Contents: When we sat in Babylon -- O Lord, turn away thy face.

JOHN ATTEY

Literature

166. Doughtie, Edward. <u>Lyrics from English airs, 1596-1622.</u>
Cambridge, Mass.: Harvard University Press, 1970. 657 p.

167. Poulton, Diana. "Attey, John." <u>The new Grove ...</u> London:
Macmillan, 1980. I:677.

      Very short biography.

168. Rimbault, Edward F. "Attey, John." <u>Grove's dictionary of
music and musicians, 5th ed.</u> New York: St. Martin's Press, 1954.
I:250-51.

      Short biography; no bibliography.

169. Warlock, Peter. <u>The English ayre.</u> London: OUP, 1926. 142 p.

      Reprint ed.: Westport, Conn.: Greenwood Press, 1970.
      Chapter 10 devoted to Attey and others.

Music

170. Attey, John. <u>The first booke of ayres of foure parts, with
tableture for the lute: so made that all the parts may be plaide
together with the lute, or one voyce with the lute and base-vyoll ...</u>
Printed by Thomas Snodham. 1622.

      RISM A/I/1 A2675.
      <u>Contents</u>: Sweet was the song -- Vain, hope, adieu -- Resound my
      voice -- Madam, for you I little grieve -- My days, my months --
      Joy, my muse -- Bright star of beauty -- My dearest and devinest

love -- Shall I tell you whom I love? -- In a grove of trees --
What is all this world but vain? -- The Gordian knot -- On a
time the amorous Silvy.

171. Attey, John. The first booke of ayres (1622). Edited by David
Greer. Menston, Eng.: Scolar Press, 1967. 37 p.

    Facsim. of the British Museum copy.
    Series: English lute songs, v. 2.
    Contents: SEE 170.

172. Attey, John. First booke of ayres, 1622. Trans., scored and ed.
from the original ed. by E. H. Fellowes. London: Stainer & Bell,
1926. 41 p.

    For solo voice, with lute accomp. trans. into modern notation
    for piano; altus, tenor and bassus parts omitted.
    Series: ESLS. Ser. 2, v. 9.
    Contents: SEE 170.

173. An Elizabethan song book: lute songs, madrigals and rounds.
Music edited by Noah Greenberg; text edited by W. H. Auden and
Chester Kallman. New York: Doubleday, 1956. 240 p.

    Contents: Sweet was the song.

174. Forty Elizabethan songs. Ed. and arr. with the original accomp.
by Edmund Horace Fellowes. London: Stainer & Bell, 1921-1926. 4 v.

    Contents: On a time the amorous silvy (v. 4)

175. Mirror of love. Ed. and trans. by Carl Shavitz. London: Chester
Music, 197-.

    Contents: My days, my months, my years.

WILLIAM BARLEY

Literature

176. Doughtie, Edward. <u>Lyrics from English airs, 1596-1622.</u>
Cambridge, Mass.: Harvard University Press, 1970. 657 p.

177. Gill, Donald. "Descriptions of the bandora, penorcon, and
orpharion from Praetorius, William Barley, Trichet MS, and Talbot MS."
<u>LSJ</u> II (1960):39ff.

178. Illing, R. "Barley's pocket edition of Est's metrical psalter."
<u>M&L</u> XLIX (1968):219-23.

179. Illing, R. "A musical trinity: Est, Barley, Ravenscroft."
<u>MT</u> CX (1969):977-78.

180. Kidson, Frank and William C. Smith. "William Barley." <u>Grove's
dictionary of music and musicians, 5th ed.</u> New York: St. Martin's
Press, 1954. I:438-39.

     Deals with William Barley as a music printer.

181. Miller, Marian. "Barley, William." <u>The new Grove ...</u> London:
Macmillan, 1980. II:162-64.

     Focuses on Barley as a publisher of music.

182. Ruff, Lillian M. "The social significance of the 17th century
English music treatises." <u>Consort</u> XXVI (1970):412.

183. Ward, John. "Barley's songs without words." <u>LSJ</u> XII (1970):5-22.

Music

184. Barley, William. A new booke of tabliture, containing sundrie
easie and familiar instructions ... Printed at London for William
Barley and are to be sold at his ship in Gratious Street. 1596.

> Contents: Thoughts make men sigh -- Love is a spirit high
> presuming -- Your face, your tongue, your wit -- Flow forth
> abundant teares -- Those eyes that set my fancy on a fire --
> Short is my rest -- How can the tree but waste and wither away.

185. Barley, William. New booke of tabliture, 1596: lute music of
Shakspeare's time. Ed. and trans. by Wilburn Newcomb. University
Park, Penn.: Pennsylvania State University Press, 1966.

> Contents: SEE 184.

JOHN BARTLET (BARTLETT)

Literature

186. Doughtie, Edward. Lyrics from English airs, 1596-1622.
Cambridge, Mass.: Harvard University Press, 1970. 657 p.

187. Fellowes, Edmund H. "John Bartlet (also Bartlett)." Grove's
dictionary of music and musicians, 5th ed. New York: St. Martin's
Press, 1954. I:463.

   Brief biography.

188. Poulton, Diana. "Bartlet, John." The new Grove ... London:
Macmillan, 1980. II:197.

   Short biographical article.

189. Warlock, Peter. The English ayre. London: OUP, 1926. 142 p.

   Reprint ed.: Westport, Conn.: Greenwood Press, 1970.
   Chapter 10 devoted to Bartlet and others.

190. Wienpahl, Robert W. "English theorists and evolving tonality."
M&L XXXVI (1955):378ff.

Music

191. Bartlet, John. A booke of ayres with a triplicitie of musicke,
whereof first part is for the lute or orpharion, and the viole de
gambo, and 4. partes to sing, the second part is for 2. trebles to
sing to the lute and viole, the third part is for the lute and one
voyce, and the viole de gambo ... Printed by John Windet, for John
Brown and are to bee solde at his shoppe in Saint Dunstones Churchyeard
in Fleet street. 1606.

RISM A/I/1 B1138.
Contents: O Lord thy faithfulness -- If ever hapless woman --
When from my love -- Who doth behold my mistress' face -- If
there be anyone -- I heard of late -- All my wits hath will
enwrapped -- Go, wailing verse -- A pretty duck there was -- Of
all the birds that I do know -- The Queen of Paphos, Ericine --
I would thou wert not fair -- Unto a fly transformed -- What
thing is love, I pray thee tell -- Fortune, love and time --
Poets to love such power ascribe -- Whither runneth my sweetheart
-- Surchanged with discontent.

192. Bartlet, John. _A booke of ayres (1606)_. Edited by David Greer.
Menston, Eng.: Scolar Press, 1967. 53 p.

Facsim. of British Museum copy.
Series: English lute songs, v. 3.
Contents: SEE 191.

193. Bartlet, John. _A booke of ayres, 1606_. London: Stainer &
Bell, 1925. 45 p.

Lute accomp. has been trans. into modern notation for piano;
bass viol is omitted.
Series: ESLS. Ser. 2, v. 3.
Contents: SEE 191.

194. _An Elizabethan song book: lute songs, madrigals, and rounds_.
Music. ed. by Noah Greenberg; text ed. by W. H. Auden and Chester
Kallman. New York: Doubleday, 1956. 240 p.

Contents: If ever haples woman -- Of all the birds -- Whither
runeth my sweethart?

195. _English ayres, Elizabethan and Jacobean_. Trans. and ed. from
the original ed. by Peter Warlock and Philip Wilson. London: OUP,
1927-31. 6 v.

Contents: Whither runneth my sweetheart? (v. 4)

196. _Forty Elizabethan songs_. Ed. and arr. with the original accomp.
by Edmund Horace Fellowes. London: Stainer & Bell, 1921-26. 4 v.

Contents: Of all the birds that I do know. (v. 1)

197. _The Oxford choral songs from the old masters_. London: OUP,
1923-29.

Contents: Who doth behold -- Whither runneth my sweetheart --
Tarry, are you gone again?

198. _What is love?_ Ed. and trans. by Carl Shavitz. London: Chester
Music, 197-.

Contents: What thing is love, I pray thee tell.

Recordings

199. <u>Elizabethan and Jacobean music</u>. Vanguard SRV 306 SD, 1971.

     Alfred Deller, countertenor; Desmond Dupré, lute; Gustav
     Leonhardt, harpsichord; Consort of Viols.
     Contents: Of all the birds that I do know.

200. <u>O ravishing delight; English songs of the 17th & 18th centuries</u>.
RCA Victrola VICS 1492, 1970.

     Also released on: Harmonia Mundi DR 215.
     Alfred Deller, counter-tenor; Desmond Dupré, lute and viola da
     gamba.
     Contents: Of all the birds that I do know.

201. <u>Wandering in this place; witty, amourous and introspective ayres
and lute solos of Elizabethan England</u>. 1750 Arch 1757, 1977.

     Contents: Unto a fly transformed from human kind.

THOMAS CAMPION

Literature

202. Auden, William H. and John Hollander. <u>Selected songs of Thomas Campion</u>. Boston: David Godine, 1973. p. 3-29.

   Includes selected song texts, music, excerpts from writings and facsimiles.

203. Barstow, Robert. The '<u>Lord Hayes masque</u>' by Thomas Campion. Unpubl. Ph.D. diss., Ohio State University, 1963. 194 p.

204. Berringer, Ralph W. "Thomas Campion's share in 'A booke of ayres.'" <u>PMLA</u> LVIII (1943):938-48.

   Suggests that Campion did not write the lyrics for Part II.

205. Campion, Thomas. <u>Songs and masques, with Observations in the art of English poesie</u>. Ed. by A. H. Bullen. London: A. H. Bullen, 1903. 288 p.

   Reprint ed.: Folcroft, Pa.: Folcroft Library Editions, 1976.
                Norwood, Pa.: Norwood Editions, 1976.

206. Campion, Thomas. <u>Campion's works</u>. Ed. by Percival Vivian. Oxford: Clarendon Press, 1909. 400 p.

   Reprint ed.: Oxford: Clarendon Press, 1966.
   An edition of poetic and prose works and includes <u>A new way of making fowre parts in counter-point</u> ... (p. 189-226). Includes biographical introduction, bibliography and list of MS sources.

207. Campion, Thomas. The works of Dr. Thomas Campion. Ed. by A. H. Bullen. London: Privately printed at the Chiswick Press, 1889. 405 p.

First collected ed.

208. Campion, Thomas. The works of Thomas Campion. Ed. with an introduction and notes by Walter R. Davis. New York: Doubleday, 1967. 521 p.

"Complete songs, masques, and treatises with a selection of the Latin verse."
Other ed.: London: Faber, 1969.
New York: Norton, 1969, 1970 (paperback)

209. Dart, Thurston. "Campion, Thomas." MGG II:728-29.

210. Davis, Walter R. "Melodic and poetic structure of Campion and Dowland." Criticism IV (1962):89-107.

211. Davis, Walter R. "Note on accent and quality in 'A book of ayres.'" MLQ XXII (1961):32-36.

212. Eldridge, Muriel T. Thomas Campion: his poetry and music (1567-1620); a study in relationships. Ph.D. diss., University of Pennsylvania, 1958. Diss. Abst. 19 (Oct. 1958):829.

213. Fellowes, Edmund H. "Thomas Campian (also Campion)" Grove's dictionary of music and musicians, 5th ed. New York: St. Martin's Press, 1954. II:32-34.

214. Finney, O. J. Thomas Campion: music and metrics. Diss. Abst. XXXVI (June 1976):4506A.

215. Flood, William H. G. "Irish ancestry of Garland, Dowland, Campion and Purcell." M&L III (1922):59-65.

216. Flood, William H. G. "New light on late Tudor composers-- XXIX. Thomas Campion." MT LXVIII (1927):895ff.

217. Gibbons, H. Observations on a 'New way of making fowre parts in counter-point' by Thomas Campion. Thesis, Harvard University, 1964.

218. Godard, John. "Such distraction of musicke; a note on the music in the masque of Thomas Campion." RMM III/7 (1968):231-33.

219. Greer, David. "Campion the musician." LSJ IX (1967):7-16.

220. Greer, David. "The part-songs of the English lutenists." PRMA XCIV (1967/68):97-110.

221. Greer, David. "Thomas Heywood's parody of a lyric by Campion." Notes and queries XII (1965):333-34.

222. Greer, David. "'What if a day'--an examination of the words and music." M&L XLIII (1962):304-19.

223. Harley, J. "Two Jacobean songs." EM VI (1978):385-89.

224. Harper, John. "A new way of making ayres? Thomas Campion: towards a revaluation." MT CX (1969):262-63.

225. Holman, P. "Introduction" to facsim. ed. of Campion, T. The description of a maske ... in honour of the Lord Hayes. Menston, Eng.: Scolar Press, 1973.

226. Holman, P. "Introduction" to facsim. ed. of Campion, T. The description of a maske ... at the mariage of the right honourable the Earle of Somerset. Menston, Eng.: Scolar Press, 1973.

227. Howard, Hubert Wendell. A man of faire parts. Ph.D. diss., University of Minnesota, 1971. Diss. Abst. XXXII (Dec. 1971):3252A.

228. Ing, Catherine. English lyrics. London: Chatto & Windus, 1951. 252 p.

    Chapter 6 is devoted to the lyrics of Campion.

229. Joiner, Mary. "Another Campion song?" M&L XLVIII (1967):138-39.

230. Kastendieck, Miles M. England's musical poet, Thomas Campion. New York: OUP, 1938. 203 p.

    Reprint ed.: 1963.
    Chapter VIII deals with Campion's music.

231. Lawrence, W. J. "Notes on a collection of masque music." M&L III (1922):49-58.

232. Lowbury, Edward, Timothy Salter and Alison Young. Thomas Campion: poet, composer, physician. London: Chatto & Windus, 1970. 195 p.

233. MacDonagh, Thomas. Campion and the art of English poetry. Dublin: Talbot Press, 1913. 128 p.

    Reprint ed.: New York: Russell & Russell, 1973.

234. Peltz, Catherine W. "Thomas Campion, an Elizabethan neoclassicist." MLQ XI (1950:3-6.

    Notes on Campion's lyrics.

235. Poulton, Diana. "Campion, Thomas." The new Grove ... London: Macmillan, 1980. III:656-660.

    Includes a list of his songs, writings and bibliography.

236. Pulver, Jeffrey. "The English theorists--XI. Thomas Campion." MT LXXV (1934):1080.

237. Ruff, Lillian M. "The social significance of the 17th century English music treatises." Consort XXVI (1970:412.

238. Sabol, Andrew J. Songs and dances for the Stuart masque.
Providence, R.I.: Brown University Press, 1959. 172 p.

"An edition of 63 items of music for the English court masque
from 1604 to 1641, with an introductory essay."
Revised ed.: Four hundred songs and dances for the Stuart
masque, 1978.

239. Shapiro, I. A. "Thomas Campion's medical degree." Notes and
queries CXCVII (1952):495.

Speculates on Campion's studies on the continent.

240. Short, R. W. "The metrical theory and practice of Thomas
Campion." PMLA LIX (1944):1003-18.

241. Sternfeld, Frederick. "A song from Campion's Lord's masque."
Journal of the Warburg and Courtauld Institutes XX (1957):373-75.

242. Swaen, A. E. H. "The authorship of 'What if a day' and its
various versions." Modern Philosophy IV (1907):397-422.

243. Vivian, Percival. "Thomas Campion." Cambridge history of English
literature IV (1909):14-19.

244. Warlock, Peter. The English ayre. London: OUP, 1926. 142 p.

Reprint ed.: Westport, Conn.: Greenwood Press, 1970.
Chapter 7 devoted to Thomas Campion.

245. Welsford, Enid. The court masque: a study in the relationship
between poetry & revels. Cambridge, Eng.: Cambridge University Press,
1927. 434 p.

Reprint ed.: New York: Russell & Russell, 1962.

246. Wienpahl, Robert W. Music at the Inns of court. Ann Arbor:
Published for the Dept. of Music, California State University,
Northridge, by University Microfilms, 1979. 309 p.

Includes a detailed account of masques at the Inns of court and
devotes a chapter to Thomas Campion.

Music

247. Campion, Thomas and Philip Rosseter. A booke of ayres, set
fourth to be song to the lute, orpherian, and base violl ... Printed
by Peter Short, by the assent of Thomas Morley. 1601.

RISM A/I/7 R2721.
Contains: My sweetest Lesbia -- Though you are young -- I care
not for these ladies -- Follow thy fair sun -- My love hath
vowed -- When to her lute Corinna sings -- Turn back you wanton
flyer -- It fell on a summer's day -- The cypress curtain of

the night -- Follow your saint -- Fair if you expect admiring
-- Thou art not fair -- See where she flies -- Blame not my
cheeks -- When the merry god of love -- Mistress, since you so
much desire -- Your fair looks -- The man of life upright --
Hark, all you ladies -- When thou must home -- Come, let us
sound with melody.

248. Campion, Thomas. A booke of ayres, 1601. Edited by David
Greer. Menston, Eng.: Scolar Press, 1970. 52 p.

> Facsim. of British Museum copy.
> Half of the songs are by Philip Rosseter.
> Series: English lute songs, v. 36.
> Contents: SEE 247.

249. Campion, Thomas. Songs from Rosseter's Book of airs, 1601.
London: Stainer & Bell, 1922-24. 2 v. (77 p.)

> Series: ESLS. Ser. 1, v. 4, 13.
> Contents: SEE 247.

250. Campion, Thomas. Songs I to X from Rosseter's Book of airs (1601).
Ed. by Edmund H. Fellowes. Revised ed. by Thurston Dart. London:
Stainer & Bell, 1959.

> Revised ed. ; original accomp. and piano accomp.
> Series: ELS. Ser. 1, v. 4.
> Contents: SEE 247.

251. Campion, Thomas. The songs from Rosseter's Book of airs (1601).
3d rev. ed. by T. Dart. London: Stainer & Bell; New York: Galaxy
Music, 1969. 2 v. in 1. (41 p.)

> Includes original lute tablature and modern notation.
> Series: ELS. Ser. 1, v. 4, 13.
> Contents: SEE 247.

252. Campion, Thomas. Two bookes of ayres. The first contayning
divine and morall songs: The second, light conceits of lovers. To
be sung to the lute and viols, in two, three, and foure parts: or by
one voyce to an instrument ... Printed by Tho. Snodham, for Mathew
Lownes, and J. Browne. (ca. 1613)

> RISM A/I/2 C626.
> Contents: BOOK I. Author of light -- The man of life upright --
> Where are all thy beauties now? -- View me, Lord, a work of
> thine -- Bravely decked, come forth -- To music bent -- Tune
> thy music to thy heart -- Most sweet and pleasing -- Wise men
> patience never want -- Never weather-beaten sail -- Lift up to
> heaven -- Lo, when back my eye -- As by the streams of Babylon --
> Sing a song of joy -- Awake, awake, thou heavy sprite -- Come
> cheerful day -- Seek the Lord -- Lighten, heavy heart, thy sprite
> -- Jack and Joan -- All looks be pale. BOOK II. Vain men whose
> follies -- How eas'ly wert thou chained -- Hardened now thy
> tired heart -- O want unhoped-for sweet supply -- Where she her
> sacred bower -- Fain would I my love disclose -- Give beauty all

her right -- O, dear, that I with thee might live -- Good men,
show if you can tell -- What harvest half so sweet is -- Sweet,
exclude me not -- The peaceful western wind -- There is none, O
none but you -- Pined I am, and liked to die -- So many loves
have I neglected -- Though your strangeness frets my heart --
Come away, armed with love's delights -- Come, you pretty false-
eyed wanton -- A secret love or two -- Her rosy cheeks -- Where
shall I refuge seek?

253. Campion, Thomas. Two bookes of ayres (ca. 1613). Ed. by David
Greer. Menston, Eng.: Scolar Press, 1967. 59 p.

    Facsim. of British Museum copy.
    Series: English lute songs, v. 4.
    Contents: SEE 252.

254. Campion, Thomas. First book of airs. Trans., scored and ed.
from the original ed. by E. H. Fellowes. London: Stainer & Bell,
1925. 29 p.

    Lute accomp. trans. from the tablature into modern notation
    for piano. Additional vocal and instrumental parts omitted.
    Series: ESLS. Ser. 2, v. 1.
    Contents: SEE 252.

255. Campion, Thomas. First book of ayres (c. 1613). Trans. and ed.
by David Scott. London: Stainer & Bell; New York: Galaxy Music,
1979. 56 p.

    For voice and lute; includes tablature.
    Contents: SEE 252.

256. Campion, Thomas. Second book of airs, circa 1613. Trans.,
scored and ed. from the original ed. by E. H. Fellowes. London:
Stainer & Bell, 1925. 39 p.

    Lute accomp. trans. from the tablature into modern notation for
    piano. Additional vocal and instrumental parts omitted.
    Series: ESLS. Ser. 2, v. 2.
    Contents: SEE 252.

257. Campion, Thomas. Second book of ayres (c. 1613). Trans. and ed.
by David Scott. London: Stainer & Bell; New York: Galaxy Music, 1979.
60 p.

    For voice and lute.
    Contents: SEE 252.

258. Campion. Thomas. The third and fourth booke of ayres: composed
... so as they may be expressed by one voyce, with a violl, lute, or
orpharion ... Printed by Thomas Snodham. (ca. 1618)

    RISM A/I/2 C627.
    Contents: BOOK III. Oft have I sighed -- Now let her change --
    Were my heart as some men's are -- Maids are simple -- So tired
    are all my thoughts -- Why presume thy pride? -- Kind are her

answers -- O grief, O spite -- O never to be moved -- Break now
my heart -- If love loves truth -- Now winter nights -- Awake,
thou spring -- What is it all? -- Fire that must flame -- If
thou long'st so much -- Shall I come, sweet love to thee? --
Thrice toss these oaken ashes -- Be thou then my beauty -- Fire,
fire! -- O sweet delight -- Thus I resolve -- Come, O come, my
life's delight -- Could my heart more tongues employ -- Sleep,
angry beauty -- Silly boy, tis full moon yet -- Never love
unless you can -- So quick, so hot, so mad -- Shall I then hope.
BOOK IV. Leave prolonging thy distress -- Respect my faith --
Thou joyest, fond boy -- Veil, love, mine eyes -- Every dame
affects good fame -- So sweet is thy discourse -- There is a
garden in her face -- To his sweet lute -- Young and simple
though I am -- Love me or not -- What means this folly? -- Dear,
if I with guile -- O love, where are thy shafts? -- Beauty is
but a painted hell -- Are you what your fair looks express? --
Since she, even she -- I must complain -- Think'st thou to seduce
me then -- Her fair inflaming eyes -- Turn all thy thoughts
to eyes -- If any hath the heart to kill -- Beauty, since you
so much desire -- Your fair looks -- Fain would I wed.

259. Campion, Thomas. The third and fourth booke of ayres, ca. 1618.
Ed. by David Greer. Menston, Eng.: Scolar Press, 1969. 48 p.

    Facsim. of British Museum copy.
    Series: English lute songs, v. 5.
    Contents: SEE 258.

260. Campion, Thomas. Third booke of ayres, circa 1617. Trans.,
scored and ed. from the original ed. by E. H. Fellowes. London:
Stainer & Bell, 1926. 55 p.

    Lute accomp. trans. from tablature into modern notation for
    piano. The bass viol part is omitted.
    Series: ESLS. Ser. 2, v. 10.
    Contents: SEE 258.

261. Campion, Thomas. Third booke of ayres (c. 1617). Ed. by Edmund
H. Fellowes. Rev. by Thurston Dart. London: Stainer & Bell; New
York: Galaxy Music, 1969. 55 p.

    Series: ELS. Ser. 2, v. 10.
    Contents: SEE 258.

262. Campion, Thomas. Fourth booke of ayres, circa 1617. London:
Stainer & Bell, 1926. 47 p.

    Series: ESLS. Ser. 2, v. 11.
    Contents: SEE 258.

263. Campion, Thomas. The discription of a maske, presented before
the Kinges Majestie at White-Hall, on twelfth night last, in honour
of the Lord Hayes, and his bride, daughter and heire to the honourable
the Lord Dennye, their marriage having been the same day at court
solemnized ... Imprinted by John Windet for John Brown and are to be
solde at his shop in S. Dunstones Churchyeard in Fleetstreet. 1607.

RISM A/I/2 C624.
Contents: Now hath Flora robb'd her bow'rs -- Move now with
measur's sound.

264. Campion, Thomas. The discription of a masque in honor of Lord
Hayes, 1607. Ed. by David Greer. Menston, Eng.: Scolar Press, 1970.
42 p.

Facsim. of the British Museum copy.
Series: English lute songs, v. 6.
Contents: SEE 263.

265. Campion, Thomas. Masque in honour of the marriage of Lord
Hayes (1607). Ed. by G. E. P. Arkwright. London: Joseph Williams;
Oxford: Parker, 1889. 15, 11 p.

Contents: SEE 263.

266. Campion, Thomas. Masque in honour of the marriage of Lord
Hayes (1607). Ed. by G. E. P. Arkwright. New York: Broude Brothers,
1968. 15, 11 p.

For solo voice with lute and bass-viol, or piano accomp.
Contents: SEE 263.

267. Campion, Thomas. The description of a maske: presented in the
banqueting roome at White-Hall, on Saint Stephens night last, at the
mariage of the right honourable the Earle of Somerset: and the right
noble the Lady Frances Howard ... Printed by E. A. for Laurence
Li'sle, dwelling in Paules Church-yard, at the signe of the tygers
head. 1614.

RISM A/I/2 C625.
Contents: Woo her and win her.

268. Campion, Thomas. The description of a masque presented at the
mariage of the Earle of Somerset, 1614. Ed. by David Greer. Menston,
Eng.: Scolar Press, 1970. 32 p.

Facsim. of the copy in the Bodleian Library.
Series: English lute songs, v. 7.
Contents: SEE 267.

269. Campion, Thomas. "Beauty is but a painted hell." Trans. and
ed. by Peter Warlock. London; Philadelphia: Curwen, (1926?) 7 p.

270. Campion, Thomas. "Break now, my heart, and die." Trans. and
ed. by Peter Warlock. London; Philadelphia: Curwen, (1926?) 7 p.

271. Campion, Thomas. "Every dame affects good fame." Trans. and ed.
by Peter Warlock. London; Philadelphia: Curwen, (1926?) 7 p.

272. Campion, Thomas. "Now let her change and spare not." Trans.
and ed. by Peter Warlock. London; Philadelphia: Curwen, (1926?). 7 p.

273. An Elizabethan song book: lute songs, madrigals and rounds.
Music ed. by Noah Greenberg; text ed. by W. H. Auden and Chester
Kallman. New York: Doubleday, 1956. 240 p.

> Contents: I care not for these ladies -- Follow thy faire sunne
> -- Turn backe you wanton flyer -- Follow your saint -- Faire,
> if you expect admiring -- Hark all you ladies -- When thou
> must home -- Never weather-beaten saile -- Jacke and Jone -- All
> lookes be pale -- What harvest halfe so sweet is -- Though your
> strangenesse frets my hart -- Kinde are her answers -- Breake
> now my heart and dye -- Now winter nights enlarge -- If thou
> longst so much to learne -- Thrice tosse these oaken ashes --
> Fire, fire -- Silly boy 'tis ful moone -- So quicke, so hot,
> so mad -- To his sweet Lute -- Thinkst thou to seduce me then.

274. English ayres, Elizabethan and Jacobean. Vol. I-VI. Trans. and
ed. from the original ed. by Peter Warlock and Philip Wilson. London:
OUP, 1927-31.

> VOL. I. Love me or not. VOL. III. Her rosy cheeks -- I care
> not for these ladies -- Shall I come, sweet love, to thee? --
> Fair, if you expect admiring. VOL. IV. There is a garden in
> her face -- Thrice toss these oaken ashes in the air -- Jack
> and Joan. VOL. V. O never to be moved -- Turn back you wanton
> flier -- Maids are simple, some men say -- Follow thy fair sun.
> VOL. VI. When to her lute Corrina sings -- Your fair looks
> inflame my desire -- Fire, fire -- Oft have I sigh'd -- So
> sweet is thy discourse to me.

275. Fire of love: songs for voice, lute and viola da gamba. Ed. and
trans. by Carl Shavitz. London: Chester Music, 1980.

> Includes a lute tablature version and a trans. version.
> Contents: Faire if you expect admiring -- Fire, loe here I
> burne -- Beauty is but a painted hell.

276. Forty Elizabethan songs. Books I-IV. Ed. and arr. with the
original accomp. by Edmund Horace Fellowes. London: Stainer & Bell,
1921-26.

> Contents: BOOK I. My sweetest Lesbia -- There is a garden in
> her face. BOOK II. Follow your saint -- When to her lute
> Corinna sings. BOOK III. The cypress curtain of the night --
> Jack and Joan. BOOK IV. Fair, if you expect admiring --
> Follow, thy fair sun.

277. Four devotional songs by Thomas Campion for mixed voices or solo
voice with accompaniment. Ed. by Kenneth Bergdolt. Macomb. Ill.:
Roger Dean, 1974. 13 p.

> Contents: Never weather-beaten sail -- Out of my soul's depth
> -- Seek the Lord -- Author of light.

278. Four hundred songs and dances from the Stuart masque. Ed. by
Andrew J. Sabol. Providence, R. I.: Brown University Press, 1978.

Contents: Now hath Flora robb'd her bow'rs -- Move now with measur'd sound -- Come away, bring thy golden theft -- Woo her and win her.

279. Mirror of love. Ed. and trans. by Carl Shavitz. London: Chester Music.

Contents: Beauty, since you so much desire -- If any hath the heart to kill -- My love hath vowed -- Sweet exclude me not.

280. The Oxford choral songs from the old masters. London: OUP, 1923-29.

Contents: Never weather-beaten sail (304) -- Tune thy music to thy heart (308) -- Wise men patience never want (308) -- To music bent is my retired mind (309) -- Thrice toss these oaken ashes in the air (309) -- There is a garden in her face (310) -- To his sweet lute Apollo sang (311) -- Jack and Joan (311) -- A man of life upright (312).

281. Selected songs of Thomas Campion. Selected and prefaced by W. H. Auden; introduction by John Hollander. Boston: D. Godine, 1973. 161 p.

For voice and lute.

Recordings

282. Altenglische Lautenlieder. Decca/Serenata 6.41648. 1960.

Title on slipcase: Lute songs - Lautenlieder - Chansons au luth. Peter Pears, tenor; Julian Bream, lute.
Contents: Come let us sound with melody -- Fair if you expect admiring -- Shall I come sweet love.

283. Ars Britannica: Old Hall Manuscript; madrigals; lute songs. Telefunken 6.35494, 1980.

Pro Cantione Antiqua.
Contents: Never weather-beaten sail -- Jack and Jone -- A secret love.

284. Character songs (by various composers). Editions de l'Oiseau lyre DSLO 545, 1980.

The Consort of Musicke; Anthony Rooley, conductor.
Contents: Jack and Joan.

285. Elizabethan and Jacobean music. Vanguard SRV 306 SD, 1971.

Alfred Deller, counter-tenor; Desmond Dupré, lute; Gustav Leonhardt, harpsichord; Consort of Viols.
Contents: I care not for these ladies.

286.   Elizabethan ayres and dances. Saga 5470, 1980.

James Bowman, counter-tenor; Robert Spencer, lute.
Contents: Fair, if you expect admiring -- Author of light --
I care not for these ladies -- The cypress curtain of the night
-- There is a garden in her face.

287.   Elizabethan lute songs and solos. Philips 6500 282, 1973.

Frank Patterson, tenor; Robert Spencer, lute.
Contents: It fell on a summer's day -- The cypress curtain
of the night -- Shall I come, sweet love to thee.

288.   English ayres and duets sung in Elizabethan pronunciation.
Hyperion A 66003, 1981.

The Camerata of London.
Contents: If thou long'st so much to learn -- Shall I come,
sweet love?

289.   English lute songs and six In nomines. Bach Guild BG-576. 1958.

Alfred Deller, counter-tenor; Desmond Dupré, lute.
Contents: Shall I come, sweet love to thee?

290.   English songs of the 16th and 17th centuries. Abbey LPB 712,
1977.

Gerald English, tenor; David Lumsden, harpsichord/ organ; Jane
Ryan, viola da gamba.
Contents: Shall I come, sweet love?

291.   Lo, country sports. Argo ZRG 658, 1971.

John Neville; James Tyler, lute; Purcell Consort of Voices;
Elizabethan Consort of Viols; Graystone Burgess, conductor.
Contents: Jack and Joan.

292.   Lutenist songs. Editions de l'Oiseau-lyre OL 50102, 1956.

Rereleased: Editions de l'Oiseau-lyre OLS 109, 1971.
Alfred Deller, counter-tenor; Desmond Dupré, lute.
Contents: Never weatherbeaten sail -- Most sweet and pleasing
are thy ways -- Author of light -- To music bent.

293.   Masque music: instrumental and vocal music from the Stuart
masque. Nonesuch H71153, 1967.

Concentus Musicus of Denmark; Aksel Mathlesen, conductor.
Contents: Now hath Flora.

294.   Music in Shakespeare's time. Concert Hall CHS 1225, 1954.

Suzanne Block accompanying herself on the lute.
Contents: Peaceful western wynd.

295. Nine songs from Rosseter's Book of ayres. Archive ARC 3004, 1955.

Rene Soames, tenor; Walter Gerwig, lute; Johannes Koch, viola da gamba.
Contents: My sweet Lesbia -- Though you are young -- I care not for these ladies -- Follow thy fair sun -- My love hath vowed -- When to her lute Corinna sings -- Turn back you wanton flyer -- It fell on a summer's day -- Follow your saint.

296. O ravishing delight: English songs of the 17th and 18th centuries. RCA Victrola VICS 1492, 1970.

Also released on: Harmonia Mundi DR 215, (197-)
Alfred Deller, counter-tenor; Desmond Dupré, lute and viola da gamba.
Contents: I care not for these ladies -- The cypress curtain of the night.

297. A pageant of English songs 1597-1961. EMI/His Master's Voice HQS 1091, 1967.

Janet Baker, mezzo soprano; Robert Spencer, lute.
Contents: Oft have I sighed -- If thou longst so much to learn -- Fain would I wed.

298. Songs, consort pieces and masque music. Meridian E 77009, 1979.

Camerata of London.
Contents: 1601. Fair if you expect admiring -- The cypress curtain of the night -- I care not for these ladies -- It fell on a summer's day. 1613. All looks be pale -- Never weather-beaten sail -- Jack and Joan -- Sweet exclude me not -- Harden now thy tired heart. 1617. Fire, fire -- What if a day -- Never love unless you can -- Fain would I wed -- So sweet is thy discourse -- What if a day. Masque music. Move now with measured sound -- Now hath Flora rob' her bowers -- While dancing rests -- Come ashore merry mates.

299. Wandering in this place; witty, amourous, and introspective ayres and lute solos of Elizabethan England. 1750 Arch 1757, 1977.

Contents: Beauty, since you so much desire.

MICHAEL CAVENDISH

Literature

300. Arnold, Denis. "Cavendish, Michael." MGG II:937-38.

301. Brown, David. "Cavendish, Michael." The new Grove ... London: Macmillan, 1980. IV:37-38.

302. Doughtie, Edward. Lyrics from English airs, 1596-1622. Cambridge, Mass.: Harvard University Press, 1970. 657 p.

303. Eitner, Robert. "Giulis Abondantes Lautenbücher." MfM VIII (1876):119-21.

304. Fellowes, Edmund H. "Michael Cavendish." Grove's dictionary of music and musicians, 5th ed. New York: St. Martin's Press, 1954. II:132-33.

   Short biography with bibliography.

305. Philipps, G. A. "John Wilbye's other patrons: the Cavendishes and their place in English musical life during the Renaissance." MusR XXXVIII (1977):81-93.

306. Warlock, Peter. The English ayre. London: OUP, 1926. 142 p.

   Reprint ed.: Westport, Conn.: Greenwood Press, 1970.
   Chapter 9 devoted to Cavendish, Greaves, Corkine, Ford,
   Pilkington, and Morley.

Music

307. Cavendish, Michael. <u>14. ayres in tabletorie to the lute expressed</u>
<u>with two voyces and the base violl or voice & lute only. 6. more to 4.</u>
<u>voyces and in tabletorie.   And 8. madrigalles to 5. voyces ...</u>
Printed by Peter Short, on Bredstreet Hill at the signe of the starre.
1598.

> RISM A/I/2 C1575.
> Contents: Stay, Glycia, stay -- Why should my muse? -- Mourn,
> Marcus, mourn -- Have I vowed and must not break it -- Finetta,
> fair and feat -- Love is not blind -- Love, the delight --
> The heart to rue -- Sylvia is fair -- Cursed be the time --
> Fair are those eyes -- Wandering in this place -- Every bush
> new springing -- Down in a valley -- Wanton, come hither --
> Say, shepherds, say -- Fair are those eyes (II) -- Farewell,
> despair -- Shy thief.

308. Cavendish, Michael. <u>14 ayres in tabletorie to the lute, 1598.</u>
Edited by David Greer. Menston, Eng.: Scolar Press, 1971. 51 p.

> Facsim. of the only surviving copy in the British Museum.
> Series: English lute songs, v. 8.
> Contents: SEE 307.

309. Cavendish, Michael. <u>Songs included in Michael Cavendish's</u>
<u>Booke of ayres and madrigalles, 1598.</u> Trans., scored and ed. from the
original ed. by Edmund H. Fellowes. London: Stainer & Bell, 1926.

> For voice and piano; originally with accomp. in lute tablature;
> no. 1-14, for solo voice or duet; no. 15-20, for four voices.
> Series: <u>ESLS</u>. Ser. 2, v. 7.
> Contents: SEE 307.

310. Cavendish, Michael. "Finetta." Trans. and ed. by Peter Warlock.
London; Philadelphia: Curwen, (1926?) 7 p.

311. Cavendish, Michael. "Wandering in this place." Trans. and ed.
by Peter Warlock. London; Philadelphia: Curwen, (1926?) 7 p.

312. <u>An Elizabethan song book: lute songs, madrigals, and rounds.</u>
Music ed. by Noah Greenberg; text ed. by W. H. Auden and Chester
Kallman. New York: Doubleday, 1956.

> Contents: Wandering in this place -- Down in a valley --
> Everie bush now springing.

313. <u>English ayres, Elizabethan and Jacobean, Vol. I-VI.</u> Trans. and
ed. from the original ed. by Peter Warlock and Philip Wilson. London:
OUP, 1927-31.

> Contents: <u>Vol. I.</u> Love is not blind -- The heart to rue.
> <u>Vol. III.</u> Love, the delight of all well-thinking minds. <u>Vol. IV.</u>
> Down in a valley. <u>Vol. V.</u> Sylvia is fair -- Curs'd be the time.
> <u>Vol. VI.</u> Mourn, Marcus, mourn.

314. Forty Elizabethan songs, Books I-IV. Ed. and arr. with original
accomp. by Edmund Horace Fellowes. London: Stainer & Bell, 1921-26.

   Contents: Book IV. Finetta, fair and feat.

315. The Oxford choral songs from the old masters. London: OUP,
1923-29.

   Contents: Down in a valley.

Recordings

316. Lo, country sports. Argo ZRG 658, 1971.

   John Neville; James Tyler, lute; Purcell Consort of Voices;
   Elizabethan Consort of Viols; Grayston Burgess, conductor.
   Contents: Down in a valley.

317. Wandering in this place; witty, amourous, and introspective
ayres and lute solos of Elizabethan England. 1750 Arch 1757, 1977.

   Contents: Wandering in this place.

JOHN COPRARIO
(COPERARIO, COOPER)

Literature

318. Aplin, J. "Sir Henry Fanshawe and two sets of early seventeenth-century part books at Christ Church, Oxford." M&L LVII (1976):11-24.

319. Charteris, Richard. "Autographs of John Coperario." M&L LVI (1975):41-46.

320. Charteris, Richard. John Coprario: a thematic catalogue of his music. New York: Pendragon Press, 1977. 113 p.

321. Charteris, Richard. "John Coprario's five- and six-part pieces: instrumental or vocal?" M&L LVII (1976):370-78.

322. Coprario, John. Rules how to compose. Los Angeles: Gottlieb, 1952. 22 p. & 41 leaves.

    "... A facsimile edition of the MS. from the library of the Earl of Bridgewater (c. 1610), now in the Huntington Library ... with an introduction by Manfred F. Bukofzer."

323. Dart, Thurston. "Coperario, Giovanni." MGG II:1658-61.

324. Dart, Thurston. "Jacobean consort music." PRMA LXXXI (1954/55): 63-75.

325. Dart, Thurston. "Music and musicians at Chichester Cathedral, 1545-1642." M&L XLII (1961):223-24.

326. Dart, Thurston. "Two English musicians at Heidelberg in 1613." MT CXI (1970):29-32.

327. Doughtie, Edward. Lyrics from English airs, 1596-1622. Cambridge, Mass.: Harvard University Press, 1970. 657.p.

328. Field, Christopher D. S. "Coprario, John." <u>The new Grove ...</u>
London: Macmillan, 1980. IV:727-30.

     Extensive bibliographical information.

329. Field, Christopher D. S. "Musical observations from Barbados
1647-50." <u>MT</u> CXV (1974):565-67.

330. Husk, William H., Jeffery Mark and Robert Donington. "John
Coperario (also Coprario and Cooper)." <u>Grove's dictionary of music
and musicians, 5th ed</u>. New York: St. Martin's Press, 1954. II:426-27.

     Biography discusses Coprario as a viola da gambist, lutenist and
     composer; includes a bibliography.

331. James, Walter Stevens. <u>John Cooper: a study of his ayres</u>.
Thesis (M.A.), University of Rochester, 1942.

332. McGrady, Richard. "Coperario's 'Funeral tears.'" <u>MusR</u> XXXVIII
(1977):163-76.

333. Ruff, Lillian M. "Dr. Blow's 'Rules for composition.'" <u>MT</u>
CIV (1963):184-85.

334. Smith, A. "The gentlemen and children of the Chapel Royal of
Elizabeth I: an annotated register." <u>RMA Research</u> V (1965):38-39.

335. Warlock, Peter. <u>The English ayre</u>. London: OUP, 1926. 142 p.

     Reprint ed.: Westport, Conn.: Greenwood Press, 1970.
     Chapter 10 is devoted to Cooper (Coprario) and others.

336. Weijers, J. J. "Coperario, Lupo en Ferrabosco, een drietal
vergeten Engelse componisten." <u>Mens en Mel</u> XXIII (1968):311-13.

<u>Music</u>

337. Coprario, Giovanni. <u>Funeral teares. For the death of the right
honorable the Earl of Devonshire. Figured in seaven songes, whereof
sixe are so set forth that the wordes may be exprest by a treble voice
alone to the lute and base viole, or else that the meane part may bee
added, if any shall affect more fulnesse of parts. The seaventh is made
in forme of a dialogue, and can not be sung without two voyces ...</u>
Printed by John Windet the assigne of William Barley, for John Browne,
and are to be sold at his shop in S. Dunstons Churchyeard in Fleet
Street. 1606.

     RISM A/I/2 C3616
     Contents: Oft thou hast -- O sweet flower -- O th'unsure hopes
     -- In darkness let me dwell -- My joy is dead -- Deceitful
     fancy -- A dialogue: Foe of mankind.

338. Coprario, John. <u>Funeral tears (1606)</u>. Edited by David Greer.
Menston, Eng.: Scolar Press, 1970. 24 p.

Facsim. of the British Museum copy.
Series: English lute songs, v. 9.
Contents: SEE 337.

339. Coprario, John. <u>Songs of mourning: bewailing the untimely death
of Prince Henry. Worded by Tho. Campion. And set forth to bee sung
with one voyce to the lute, or violl ...</u> Printed by John Browne, and
are to be sould in S. Dunstons Churchyard. 1613.

RISM A/I/2 C3617.
Contents: O grief -- Tis now dead night -- Fortune and glory --
So parted you -- How like a golden dream -- When pale famine --
O poor distracted world.

340. Coprario, John. <u>Songs of mourning (1613)</u>. Menston, Eng.:
Scolar Press, 1970. 24 p.

Facsimile of the copy in the Bodleian Library (Mus. 5d 899).
Series: English lute songs, v. 10.
Contents: SEE 339.

341. Coprario, John. <u>Funeral tears (1606), Songs of mourning (1613)
(and) The masque of squires (1614)</u>. Trans. and ed. by Gerald Hendrie
and Thurston Dart. London: Stainer & Bell; New York: Galaxy Music,
1959. 43 p.

For 1-2 voices and piano, also includes original lute tablature.
Series: ELS. Ser. 1, v. 17.
Contents: <u>Funeral tears</u> SEE 337.
         <u>Songs of mourning</u> SEE 339.
         <u>The masque of squires</u>. Go happy man -- While dancing
rests -- Come ashore merry mates -- Send home my long-stray'd
eyes.

342. <u>English ayres, Elizabethan and Jacobean. Vol. I-VI</u>. Trans. and
ed. from the original ed. by Peter Warlock and Philip Wilson. London:
OUP, 1927-31.

Contents: <u>Vol. IV</u>. O sweet flower. <u>Vol. V</u>. So parted you.

343. <u>The Oxford choral songs from the old masters</u>. London: OUP,
1923-29.

Contents: O sweet flower (no. 302).

Recordings

344. Coprario, John. <u>Funeral teares: Consort music</u>. Editions de
l'Oiseau-lyre DSLO 576, 1981.

The Consort of Musicke; Anthony Rooley, director.
Contents: SEE 337.

345. Coprario, John. <u>Songs of mourning: Consort music</u>. Editions de
l'Oiseau-lyre DSLO 511, 1977.

    Martyn Hill, tenor; Consort of Musicke, Anthony Rooley, director.
    Contents: SEE 339.

346. <u>Masque music: instrumental and vocal music from the Stuart
Masque</u>. Nonesuch H71153, 1967.

    Concentus Musicus of Denmark; Aksel Mathlesen, conductor.
    Contents: While dancing rests -- Come ashore -- The squire's
    masque.

WILLIAM CORKINE

Literature

347. Boetticher, Wolfgang. "Corkine, William." <u>MGG</u> II:1679-80.

348. Doughtie, Edward. <u>Lyrics from English airs, 1596-1622</u>. Cambridge, Mass.: Harvard University Press, 1970. 657 p.

349. Husk, William H. "William Corkine." <u>Grove's dictionary of music and musicians, 5th ed</u>. New York: St. Martin's Press, 1954. II:441.

   Brief biography.

350. Poulton, Diana. "Corkine, William." <u>The new Grove ...</u> London: Macmillan, 1980. IV:779.

351. Warlock, Peter. <u>The English ayre</u>. London: OUP, 1926. 142 p.

   Reprint ed.: Westport, Conn.: Greenwood Press, 1970.
   Chapter 9 is devoted to Corkine and others.

Music

352. Corkine, William. <u>Ayres, to sing and play to the lute and basse violl. With pavins, galliards, almaines, and corantos for the lyra violl</u> ... Printed by W. Stansby for John Browne, and are to be sold at his shop in Saint Dunstanes Church-yard in Fleete-streete. 1610.

   RISM A/I/2 C3936.
   Contents: Sink down, proud thoughts -- Some can flatter -- Sweet, restrain these showers -- If streams of tears -- Sweet, let me go -- He that hath no mistress -- Sweet Cupid -- Vain is all this world's contention -- Beauty sat bathing -- Now would

'chwore hong'd -- Think you to seduce me so -- Shall a frown or angry eye?

353. Corkine, William. <u>Ayres to sing and play to the lute, 1610</u>.   Ed. by David Greer. Menston, Eng.: Scolar Press, 1970.

    Facsim. of the copy in British Museum (K.8h.4).
    Series: English lute songs, v. 11.
    Contents: SEE 352.

354. Corkine, William. <u>First book of ayres, 1610</u>. Trans., scored and ed. from the original ed. by E. H. Fellowes. London: Stainer & Bell, 1926. 23 p.

    Lute tablature trans. into modern notation for piano; bass
    viol part omitted.
    Series: ESLS. Ser. 2, v. 12.
    Contents: SEE 352.

355. Corkine, William. <u>The second booke of ayres, some, to sing and play to the base-violl alone: others to be sung to the lute and base-violl. With new corantoes, pavins, almains; and also divers new descants upon old grounds, set to the lyra-violl</u> ... Printed for M. L. I. B. and T. S. Assigned by W. Barley. 1612.

    RISM A/I/2 C3937.
    Contents: Each lovely grace -- Truth-trying time -- Two lovers
    sat lamenting -- 'Tis true 'tis day -- Dear, though your mind --
    Shall I be with joys deceived? -- Down, down, proud mind --
    Beware, fair maids -- The fire to see my woes -- Go, heavy
    thoughts -- My dearest mistress -- Man, like a prophet --
    As by a fountain -- Away, away! call back -- When I was born --
    Shall a smile or guileful glance? -- We yet agree -- Fly swift,
    my thoughts.

356. Corkine, William. <u>The second booke of ayres (1612)</u>. Ed. by David Greer. Menston, Eng.: Scolar Press, 1970. 40 p.

    Facsim. of British Museum copy.
    Series: English lute songs, v. 12.
    Contents: SEE 355.

357. Corkine, William. <u>Second booke of ayres, 1612</u>. London: Stainer & Bell, 1927. 47 p.

    Bass viol accomp. realized for piano.
    Series: ESLS. Ser. 2, v. 13.
    Contents: SEE 355.

358. Corkine, William. "Truth-trying time." Trans., and ed. by Peter Warlock. London; Philadelphia: Curwen, (1926?) 5 p.

359. <u>An Elizabethan song book: lute songs, madrigals, and rounds</u>. Music ed. by Noah Greenberg; text ed. by W. H. Auden and Chester Kallman. New York: Doubleday, 1956.

Contents: Two lovers sat lamenting.

360. <u>English ayres, Elizabethan and Jacobean. Vol. I-VI</u>. Trans. and ed. from the original ed. by Peter Warlock and Philip Wilson. London: OUP, 1927-31.

Contents: <u>Vol. I</u>. Shall a frown or angry eye? <u>Vol. III</u>. Sweet let me go. <u>Vol. V</u>. Beauty sat bathing.

361. <u>Forty Elizabethan songs</u>. Books I-IV. Ed. and arr. with the original accomp. by Edmund Horace Fellowes. London: Stainer & Bell, 1921-26.

Contents: <u>Book I</u>. Down, down, proud mind.

362. <u>Mirror of love</u>. Ed. and trans. by Carl Shavitz. London: Chester Music, 197-?

Contents: Away, away -- He that hath no mistress -- Two lovers sat lamenting.

JOHN DANYEL (DANIEL)

Literature

363. Arnold, Denis. "Danyel, John." <u>MGG</u> II:1892-93.

364. Doughtie, Edward. <u>Lyrics from English airs, 1596-1622</u>. Cambridge, Mass.: Harvard University Press, 1970. 657 p.

365. Fellowes, Edmund H. "John Daniel (also Danyel)." <u>Grove's dictionary of music and musicians, 5th ed</u>. New York: St. Martin's Press, 1954. II:591-92.

    Short biography with bibliography.

366. Flood, William H. "New light on late Tudor composers--XXXII. John Daniel." <u>MT</u> LXIX (1928):218.

367. Harner, James L. <u>Samuel and Daniel and Michael Drayton: a reference guide</u>. Boston: G. K. Hall, 1980. 338 p.

    An annotated bibliography to Samuel Daniel, the poet and brother of John Danyel. Provides citations and biographical information.

368. Judd, Percy. "The songs of John Danyel." <u>M&L</u> XVII (1936):118-23.

369. Lindley, David. "John Danyel's 'Eyes looke no more'." <u>LSJ</u> XVI (1974)9-16.

370. Lumsden, David. <u>The sources of English lute music, 1540-1620</u>. Unpubl. Ph.D. diss., University of Cambridge, 1955. 3 v.

371. Rees, Joan. <u>Samuel Daniel: a critical and biographical study</u>. Liverpool: Liverpool University Press, 1964. 183 p.

372. Rooley, Anthony. "The lute solos and duets of John Danyel."
LSJ XIII (1971):18-27.

373. Scott, David. "Danyel, John." _The new Grove_ ... London:
Macmillan, 1980. III:233-34.

374. Scott, David. "John Danyel: his life and songs." _LSJ_ XIII
(1971):7-17.

375. Sellers, Harry. "Samuel Daniel: additions to the text."
Modern Language Review XI (January 1916):28-32.

   Draws attention to two versions of Delia sonnets in John
   Danyel's _Songs for the lute_.

376. Swanekamp, Joan. _The English ayres of John Danyel_. Unpubl.
Master's thesis, University of Miami, Florida, 1975. 83 p.

   Includes biographical information and an analysis of Danyel's
   1606 book of ayres.

377. Warlock, Peter. _The English ayre_. London: OUP, 1926. 142 p.

   Reprint ed.: Westport, Conn.: Greenwood Press, 1970.
   Chapter 3 is devoted to Danyel.

378. Warlock, Peter. "John Danyel--music." _MT_ LXVI (1925):314ff.

Music

379. Danyel, John. _Songs for the lute, viol and voice_ ... Printed by
T. E. for Thomas Adams, at the signe of the white lyon, in Paules
Church-yard. 1606.

   RISM A/I/2 D906.
   Contents: Coy Daphne fled -- Thou pretty bird -- He whose
   desires are still abroad -- Like as the lute delights -- Dost
   thou withdraw thy grace? -- Why canst thou not? -- Stay, cruel,
   stay -- Time, cruel time -- Grief keep within -- Let not
   Cloris think -- Can doleful notes? -- Eyes, look no more --
   If I could shut the gate -- I die whenas I do not see -- What
   delights can thou enjoy? -- Now the earth, the skies, the air.

380. Danyel, John. _Songs for the lute (1606)_. Ed. by David Greer.
Menston, Eng.: Scolar Press, 1970. 48 p.

   Facsim. of copy in the British Museum (K.2.g.9).
   Series: English lute songs, v. 13.
   Contents: SEE 379.

381. Danyel, John. _Songs for the lute, viol and voice (1606)_.
Ed. by E. H. Fellowes. London: Stainer & Bell, 1926. 60 p.

Original lute tablature trans. from tablature into modern
notation for piano; viol part omitted.
Series: ESLS. Ser. 2, v. 8.
Contents: SEE 379.

382. Danyel, John. Songs for the lute, viol and voice (1606). Ed.
by E. H. Fellowes; revised under the direction of Thurston Dart; this
volume revised by David Scott. London: Stainer & Bell; New York:
Galaxy Music, 1970. 77 p.

Accomp. ed. from lute tablature for keyboard instrument.
Series: ELS. Ser. 2, v. 8.
Contents: SEE 379.

383. Danyel, John. "He whose desires are still abroad (1606)."
Trans. and ed. by Peter Warlock. London; Philadelphia: Curwen,
(1926?). 7 p.

384. An Elizabethan song book: lute songs, madrigals, and rounds.
Music ed. by Noah Greenberg; text ed. by W. H. Auden and Chester
Kallman. New York: Doubleday, 1956.

Contents: Tyme, cruel, time.

385. English ayres, Elizabethan and Jacobean. Vol. I-VI. Trans. and
ed. from the original ed. by Peter Warlock and Philip Wilson. London:
OUP, 1927-31.

Contents: Vol. I. Coy Daphne. Vol. III. Why canst thou not as
others do? -- Stay, cruel, stay. Vol. IV. Time, cruel, time.
Vol. V. Thou pretty bird -- Let not Cloris think -- Dost thou
withdraw thy grace? -- If I could shut the gate against my
thoughts. Vol. VI. Mrs. M. E. her funeral tears -- Eyes look
no more.

386. Fire of love: songs for voice, lute and viola da gamba. Ed. and
trans. by Carl Shavitz. London: Chester Music, 1980.

Contents: Dost thou withdraw thy grace?

Recordings

387. Danyel, John. Lute songs 1606. Editions de l'Oiseau-lyre
DSLO 568, 1981.

The Consort of Musicke; Anthony Rooley, director.
Contents: SEE 379.

388. Danyel, John. Songs for the lute, viol and voice, 1606. Aurora
AUR 7001, 1979.

London Music Players, Martin Cole, director.
Contents: SEE 379.

389. Elizabethan ayres and dances. Saga 5470, 1980.

      James Bowman, counter-tenor; Robert Spencer, lute.
      Contents: Eyes, look no more -- Like as the lute delights --
      What delight can they enjoy?

390. English ayres and duets sung in authentic Elizabethan pronunciation.
Hyperion A66003, 1981.

      The Camerata of London.
      Contents: Eyes look no more.

391. English lute songs and six In nomines. Bach Guild BG-576, 1958.

      Alfred Deller, counter-tenor; Desmond Dupre, lute.
      Contents: Chromatic tunes.

392. English songs of the 16th and 17th centuries. Abbey LPB 712,
1977.

      Gerald English, tenor; David Lumsden, harpsichord/organ; Jane
      Ryan, viola da gamba.
      Contents: Dost thou withdraw thy grace?

393. Late sixteenth century music (part II). Pleiades Records
P256, 1973.

      University of Chicago Collegium Musicum.
      Contents: Stay, cruel, stay.

394. Musik fur Kaiser, König Bettelmann. RCA RL 25140, 1978.

      Paul Elliott, tenor; Geoffrey Shaw, baritone; The London Early
      Music Group.
      Contents: Tyme, cruell, tyme.

395. What pleasures have great princes: William Byrd and his contemporaries. RCA Red Seal CRL 2-2794, 1977.

      The London Early Music Group.
      Contents: Tyme, cruell, tyme.

JOHN DOWLAND

Literature

396. Brown, Patricia. "Influences on the early lute songs of John Dowland." Musicology (Australia) III (1968/69):21-33.

397. Chapman, E. "Dowland's quarter-centenary." Mus Events XVIII (November 1963):22ff.

398. Chazanoff, D. "English Renaissance string writing (1575-1625)." AST XVIII/3 (1968):31ff.

399. Dart, Thurston. "Dowland, John." MGG III:717-22.

400. Dart, Thurston. "John Dowland and his music." The Listener no. 1264 (1963):858ff.

401. Davis, Walter R. "Melodic and poetic structure of Campion and Dowland." Criticism IV (1962):89-107.

402. Doughtie, Edward. Lyrics from English airs, 1596-1622. Cambridge, Mass.: Harvard University Press, 1970. 657 p.

403. Doughtie, Edward. "Nicholas Breton and two songs by Dowland." RenaisN XVII (1964):1-3.

404. Doughtie, Edward. Poems from the songbooks of John Dowland. Unpubl. Ph.D. diss., Harvard University, 1963.

405. Dowling, Margaret. "The printing of John Dowland's 'Second book of songs or ayres'." The Library 4th ser. XII (1932/33):365-90.

406. Fellowes, Edmund H. "The songs of John Dowland." PRMA LVI (1929-30):1-26.

407. Flood, William H. G. "Irish ancestory of Garland, Dowland, Campion and Purcell." M&L III (1922):59-65.

408. Flood, William H. G. "New facts about John Dowland." Gentleman's Magazine (1906):287-91.

409. Flood, William H. G. "New light on late Tudor composers--XXV. John Dowland." MT LXVIII (1927):504ff.

410. Gable, F. K. "Two songs in Shakespeare's 'Twelfth night'--suggestions for practical performance." Am Rec XIX (1978):52-56.

411. Goins, Eddie T. John Dowland and the art song. Unpubl. Ph.D. diss., University of Iowa, 1962. Diss. Abst. XXIII (Feb. 1963): 2934-35.

412. Greer, David. "The part songs of the English lutenists." PRMA XCIV (1967/68):97-110.

413. Hammerich, Angul. "Musical relations between England and Denmark in the seventeenth century." SIMG XIII (1911/12):114-19.

414. Henning, Rudolf. "A possible source of Lachrimae?" LSJ XIV (1974):65-67.

415. Hill, Cecil. "Dowland." MT CV (1964):199ff.

416. Hill, Cecil. "John Dowland: some new facts and a quartercentenary tribute." MT CIV (1963):785-87.

417. Jacobson, B. "Dowland 400th (concert by Julian Bream)." Mus & Mus XII (December 1963):41ff.

418. Jeffery, Brian. "Anthony Holborne." MD XXII (1968):129-65.

419. Johnson, Francis. "Printer's copy books and the black market in the Elizabethan book trade." The Library 5th ser. I (1946):97-105.

420. Jorgens, Elsie Bickford. "Sweet stay awhile: six music interpretations." Centerpoint II (1977):1-10.

421. Kingsley, N. "Do the words matter?" Consort XXV (1968/69): 396-404.

422. Klessman, Eckart. "Die Deutschlandreise John Dowlands." Musica XI (1957):13-15.

423. Klessman, Eckart. "Die Italienreise John Dowlands." Musica XI (1957):320-22.

424. Klessman, Eckart. "John Dowland." Hausmusik XIII (1959):10-14.

425. Klessman, Eckart. "Die letzten Jahre John Dowlands." Musica XII (1958):390-94.

426. Lowinski, E. Tonality and atonality in sixteenth century music. Berkeley; Los Angeles: University of California Press, 1961. p. 54-61.

427. Manning, Rosemary. "Lachrimaè: a study of John Dowland." M&L XXV (1944):44-53.

428. Mies, Otto. "Dowland's Lachrymaè tune." MD IV (1950):59-64.

429. Mies, Otto. "Elizabethan music prints in an East Prussian castle." MD III (1949):171-72.

    Briefly notes rare copies of early editions of works by John and Robert Dowland and Robert Jones.

430. Nagel, Wilibald. "John Doüland's necessarie observations belonging to lute-playing (German translation of and commentary on R. Dowland's Varietie ... (1610))" MfM XXIII (1891):145-62.

431. "Notes of the day (Music Britannica has not forgotten Dowland)" MMR LXXXI (1951):175-80.

432. "Notes on phonograph recordings; fifteen songs by John Dowland (review of recording)." RenaisN IV (summer 1951):29-30.

433. Poulton, Diana. "The burial of John Dowland." LSJ IV (1962):32ff.

434. Poulton, Diana. "The Dolmetsch Library, Haslemere, MS II B.1, a preliminary study." Consort XXXV (1979):327-41.

435. Poulton, Diana. "Dowland, John." The new Grove ... London: Macmillan, 1980. V:593-97.

    A list of his vocal and instrumental works is included.

436. Poulton, Diana. "Dowland's songs and their instrumental forms." MMR LXXXI (1959):175-80.

437. Poulton, Diana. John Dowland. London: Faber, 1972. 520 p.

    2d ed.: 1982. 528 p.

438. Poulton, Diana. "John Dowland." MT CV (1964):275-76.

439. Poulton, Diana. "John Dowland; a reply to Hill ..." MT CV (1964):25-27.

440. Poulton, Diana. "John Dowland and Elizabethan melancholy." RMM IV (1969):40-42.

441. Poulton, Diana. "John Dowland, Doctor of Music." Consort XX (1963):189-97.

442. Poulton, Diana. "John Dowland's patrons and friends." LSJ IV (1963):7-17.

443. Poulton, Diana. "John Dowland's songs and their instrumental forms." MMR LXXXI (1951):175-80.

444. Poulton, Diana. "Lady Hunsden's puffes." MT CV (1964):518ff.

445. Poulton, Diana. "The lute music of John Dowland." Consort VIII (1950):10-15.

446. Poulton, Diana. "Was John Dowland a singer?" LSJ VI (1965):32-37.

447. Priebe, J. "You really should know Dowland." Repertoire I (1951):31ff.

448. Richardson, Brian. "New light on Dowland's continental movements." MMR XC (1960):3-9.

449. "Robert Douland's Musical banquet, 1610." MA I (1910):45-55.

450. Rooley, Anthony. "John Dowland and English lute music." EM III (1975):115-118.

451. Sharp, G. "English composers abroad." Church Music (London) II (1968):5.

452. Smith, James G. John Dowland; a reappraisal of his ayres. Unpubl. D.M.A. thesis, University of Illinois, Urbana, 1973. 457 p. Diss. Abst. XXXIV (Mar. 1974):6030A.

453. Spencer, R. "Three English lute manuscripts." EM III (1975):122-24.

454. Squire, William Barclay and Edmund H. Fellowes. "John Dowland." Grove's dictionary of music and musicians, 5th ed. New York: St. Martin's Press, 1954. II:754-58.

    Biography and bibliography.

455. Squire, William Barclay. "John Dowland." MT XXXVII (1896): 792-94, XXXVIII (1897):92-93.

456. Swan, A. J. "John Dowland." GR (1949):13ff.

457. Ward, John. "Communications (Errata and addenda to his monograph A Dowland Miscellany)" JLSA XI (1978):101ff.

458. Ward, John. "A Dowland miscellany (additions to John Dowland: his life and works, by Diana Poulton; and Collected lute music of John Dowland, ed. by D. Poulton and B. Lam)" JLSA X (1977):5-153.

459. Warlock, Peter. The English ayre. London: OUP, 1926. 142 p.

    Reprint ed.: Westport, Conn.: Greenwood Press, 1970.
    Chapter 2 devoted to Dowland.

460. Warlock, Peter. "More light on John Dowland." MT LXVIII (1927): 689-91.

461. Warlock, Peter. "A note on John Dowland." MT LXVII (1926):209ff.

462. Weed, Jane Spangenberg. The airs of John Dowland. Thesis (M.A.),
University of Rochester, 1958.

463. Wells, Robin H. "The art of persuasion (Come again/Dowland)."
LSJ XIV (1974):67-69.

Music

464. Dowland, John. The first booke of songes or ayres of fowre partes
with tableture for the lute: so made that all partes together, or either
of them severally may be song to the lute, orpherian or viol de gambo ...
Also an invention by the sayd author for two to playe upon one lute ...
Printed by Peter Short, dwelling on Bredstreet Hill at the sign of the
starre, 1597.

    RISM A/I/2 D3478.
    Contents: Unquiet thoughts -- Who ever thinks or hopes of love
    for love -- My thoughts are winged with hopes -- If my complaints
    could passions move -- Can she excuse my wrongs with virtue's
    cloak? -- Now, O now, I needs must part -- Dear, if you change
    I'll never choose again -- Burst forth, my tears -- Go, crystal
    tears -- Think'st thou then by thy feigning? -- Come away, come,
    sweet love! -- Rest awhile, you cruel cares -- Sleep, wayward
    thoughts -- All ye, whom love or fortune -- Wilt thou, unkind,
    thus reave me? -- Would my conceit -- Come again! Sweet love
    doth now invite -- His golden locks -- Awake sweet love, thou
    art returned -- Come, heavy sleep -- Away with these self-loving
    lads.

465. Dowland, John. The first booke of songes or ayres (1597). Ed.
by Diana Poulton. Menston, Eng.: Scolar Press, 1968. 53 p.

    Facsim. ed. of British Museum copy.
    Series: English lute songs, v. 14.
    Contents: SEE 464.

466. Dowland, John. First book of airs 1597. Trans., scored and ed.
by E. H. Fellowes. London: Stainer & Bell, 1920-21. 2 v.

    Two versions for each song are given: one with lute accomp. in
    modern notation and in tablature, and one with accomp. arr. for
    piano. Altus, tenor and bassus parts are omitted.
    Series: ESLS. Ser. 1, v. 1-2.
    Contents: SEE 464.

467. Dowland, John. The first book of ayres (1597, 1600, 1603, 1606,
1613). Ed. by E. Fellowes; rev. by Thurston Dart. London: Stainer &
Bell; New York: Galaxy Music, 1965. 2 v. in 1.

    Rev. ed.; for voice and lute with piano trans.
    Based on the ed. of 1606 and 1613.
    Series: ELS. Ser. 1, v. 1-2.
    Contents: SEE 464.

468. Dowland, John. <u>The first booke of songs or ayres of four parts</u>.
Ed. by William Chappell. London: Musical Antiquarian Society, n.d.
91 p.

Contents: SEE 464.

469. Dowland, John. <u>The first booke of songs (1613)</u>. Ed. by Diana
Poulton. Menston, Eng.: Scolar Press, 1968. 53 p.

Facsim. of the British Museum copy.
Series: English lute songs, v. 15.
Contents: SEE 464.

470. Dowland, John. <u>The second booke of songs or ayres, of 2. 4. and</u>
<u>5. parts: with tableture for the lute or orpherian, with the violl de</u>
<u>gamba ... also an excelent lesson for the lute and base viol, called</u>
<u>Dowland's adew</u> ... Printed by Thomas Este, the assigne of Thomas
Morley. 1600.

RISM A/I/2 D3483.
Contents: I saw my lady weep -- Flow, my tears -- Sorrow, stay --
Die not before thy day -- Mourn, day is with darkness fled --
Time's eldest son, old age -- Then sit thee down and say --
When others sing Venite -- Praise blindness, eyes -- O sweet
woods -- If floods of tears -- Fine knacks for ladies -- Now
cease my wandering eyes -- Come ye heavy states of night --
White as lilies was her face -- Woeful heart -- A shepherd in
a shade -- Faction that ever dwells -- Shall I sue? -- Toss not
my soul -- Clear or cloudy -- Humour, say what mak'st thou here?

471. Dowland, John. <u>The second booke of songes or ayres (1600)</u>.
Ed. by Diana Poulton. Menston, Eng.: Scolar Press, 1970. 54 p.

Facsim. ed. of copy in the Folger Shakespeare Library, Washington,
D.C.
Series: English lute songs, v. 16.
Contents: SEE 470.

472. Dowland, John. <u>Second book of airs (1600)</u>. Trans., scored and
ed. from the original ed. by E. H. Fellowes. London: Stainer & Bell,
1922. 2 v.

Two versions of each song are given: one with lute accomp. in
modern notation and in tablature, and one with accomp. arr. for
piano.
Series: ESLS. Ser. 1, v. 5-6.
Contents: SEE 470.

473. Dowland, John. <u>The second booke of songs (1600)</u>. Ed. by E.
Fellowes; rev. by Thurston Dart. London: Stainer & Bell; New York:
Galaxy Music, 1969. 2 v. in 1.

Rev. ed.; principally for voice and lute (tablature) with piano.
Series: ELS. Ser. 1, v. 5-6.
Contents: SEE 470.

474. Dowland, John. The third and last booke of songs or aires.
Newly composed to sing to the lute, orpharion, or viols, and a dialogue
for a base and meane lute with five voices to sing thereto ... Printed
at London by P.S. for Thomas Adams, and are to be sold at the signe
of the white lion in Paules Church-yard, by the assignment of a
patent granted to T. Morley. 1603.

> RISM A/I/2 D3484.
> Contents: Farewell, too fair -- Time stands still -- Behold
> a wonder here -- Daphne was not so chaste -- Me, me, and none
> but me -- When Phoebus first did Daphne love -- Say, love, if
> ever thou didst find -- Flow not so fast, ye fountains -- What
> if I never speed? -- Love stood amazed -- Lend your ears to my
> sorrow -- By a fountain where I lay -- O what hath overwrought?
> -- Farewell, unkind! -- Weep you no more sad fountains -- Fie
> on this feigning -- I must complain -- It was a time when silly
> bees -- The lowest trees have tops -- What poor astronomers are
> they -- Come when I call.

475. Dowland, John. The third and last booke of songs or ayres (1603).
Menston, Eng.: Scolar Press, 1970. 52 p.

> Facsim. of the copy in the Folger Shakespeare Library, Washington,
> D.C.
> Series: English lute songs, v. 17.
> Contents: SEE 474.

476. Dowland, John. Third book of airs (1603). Trans., scored and ed.
by E. H. Fellowes. London: Stainer & Bell, 1923. 2 v.

> Two versions of each song are given: one with lute accomp. in
> modern notation and tablature, and one with accomp. arr. for
> piano.
> Series: ESLS. Ser. 1, v. 10-11.
> Contents: SEE 474.

477. Dowland, John. Third book of airs (1603). London: Stainer &
Bell; New York: Galaxy Music, 1961-62. 2 v.

> Series: ELS. Ser. 1, v. 10-11.
> Contents: SEE 474.

478. Dowland, John. The third book of airs (1603). Ed. by E. Fellowes;
Rev. ed. by David Scott. London: Stainer & Bell; New York: Galaxy
Music, 1970. 2 v. in 1.

> 2d rev. ed.; for voice and lute (tablature) with piano transcription.
> Series: ELS. Ser. 1, v. 10-11.
> Contents: SEE 474.

479. Dowland, John. A pilgrimes solace. Wherein is contained musicall
harmonie of 3. 4. and 5. parts, to be sung and plaid with the lute and
viols ... Printed for M.L., J.B. and T.S. by the assignment of William
Barley. 1612.

RISM A/I/2 D3486.
Contents: Disdain me still -- Sweet, stay awhile -- To ask for
all thy love -- Love those beams that breed -- Shall I strive
with words to move? -- Were every thought an eye -- Stay, time,
awhile thy flying -- Tell me, true love -- Go nightly cares --
From silent night -- Lasso vita mia -- In this trembling shadow
cast -- If that a sinner's sighs -- To mighty God -- Where sin
sore wounding -- My heart and tongue were twins -- Up, merry
mates, to Neptune's praise -- Welcome, black night -- Cease
these false sports.

480. Dowland, John. A pilgrimes solace ... (1612). Menston, Eng.:
Scolar Press, 1970. 52 p.

   Facsim. of the copy in the Folger Shakespeare Library, Washington,
   D.C.
   Series: English lute songs, v. 19.
   Contents: SEE 479.

481. Dowland, John. A pilgrimes solace (Fourth book of airs) 1612.
Trans., scored and ed. from the original ed. by E. H. Fellowes.
London: Stainer & Bell, 1924-25. 2 v.

   Vol. 2 has the subtitle: And three songs included in A musicall
   banquet, 1610.
   Two versions are given for most of the songs; one with original
   lute accomp. in modern notation and in tablature, and one with
   accomp. arr. for piano.
   Series: ESLS. Ser. 1, v. 12, 14.
   Contents: SEE 479.

482. Dowland, John. A pilgrimes solace (1612); Three songs from A
Musicall banquet (1610). Ed. by E. H. Fellowes; revised by Thurston
Dart. London: Stainer & Bell; New York: Galaxy Music, 1969. 86 p.

   Rev. ed.; original accomp. is printed both in lute tablature and
   modern notation. Also includes parts for treble viol (violin)
   and bass viol (violoncello) for nos. 9-11.
   Series: ELS. Ser. 1, v. 12, 14.
   Contents: SEE 479.

483. Dowland, John. Ayres for four voices. Trans. by Edmund H.
Fellowes; ed. by Thurston Dart and Nigel Fortune. Published for the
Royal Musical Association. London: Stainer & Bell, 1953. 115 p.

   For SATB and lute in modern notation; in part with soprano
   solo and 2d lute.
   2d rev. ed.: 1963, 1970.

484. Dowland, John. Come again! Sweet love doth now invite. Ed.
by E. H. Fellowes; tonic solfa translation by H. J. Timothy. London:
Stainer & Bell, 1925. 4 p.

   For chorus (SATB).

485. Dowland, John. <u>English lute songs by John Dowland</u>. With the
original lute tablature and guitar transcriptions, selected, edited
and made by Brian Jeffery. London: Tecla Editions, 1982.

    Contents: Come again, sweet love doth now invite -- Sleep,
    wayward thoughts -- Awake, sweet love -- Flow my tears -- I
    saw my lady weep -- Shall I sue? -- Flow not so fast, ye
    fountains -- Say, love, if ever thou didst find -- Sweet, stay
    awhile -- To ask for all thy love -- Stay, time, awhile thy
    flying -- Time stands still.

486. Dowland, John. <u>English lute songs</u>. With the original lute
tablature and guitar transcriptions; selected, ed., and guitar trans.
made by Brian Jeffery. New York: Shattinger International, 1977. 32 p.

    Contents: SEE 485.

487. Dowland, John. <u>Fifty songs selected from works of John Dowland</u>.
Trans., scored and ed. from the original ed. by E. H. Fellowes.
London: Stainer & Bell, 1925. 2 v.

488. Dowland, John. <u>Fifty songs</u>. Selected and ed. by Edmund H.
Fellowes. Rev. with a new preface by David Scott. London: Stainer &
Bell; New York: Galaxy Music, 1971. 2 v.

489. Dowland, John. <u>In praise of Cynthia - Cynthia zu loben: airs
for four voices</u>. Ed. by Percy M. Young. Leipzig: VEB Deutscher
Verlag für Musik, 1977.

    Contents: Now, O now, I needs must part -- Go, chrystal tears --
    Away with these self-loving lads -- Come, heavy sleep -- His
    golden locks -- Come again, sweet love.

490. Dowland, John. <u>Lieder mit Klavierbegleitung - Songs with piano</u>.
Lautentabulatur übertragen und bearb. von Karl Scheit; Deutsche Nach-
dichtung der Liedertexte von Frantz Krieg. Wien: Universal, 1957. 20 p.

    Contents: Go crystal tears -- Wilt thou unkind, thus reave me --
    Come again -- Awake sweet love -- Come, heavy sleep -- Away
    with these self-loving lads -- If my complaints.

491. Dowland, John. <u>Six songs</u>. Arr. by Desmond Dupré for voice and
guitar. London: Schott, 1954. 10 p.

    Contents: I saw my lady weep -- Fine knacks for ladies -- What
    if I never speed -- In darkness let me dwell -- Flow, my
    tears -- Come away, come, sweet love.

492. Dowland, John. <u>Sweet stay awhile: four-part ayres selected from
volume 6 of Musica Britannica</u>. Trans. by Edmund H. Fellowes; and ed.
by Thurston Dart and Nigel Fortune. London: Stainer & Bell; New York:
Galaxy, 1976.

    Contents: Come again -- If my complaints -- Now, oh now, I
    needs must part -- Come away, come sweet love -- Burst forth,
    my tears -- Go, crystal tears -- Can she excuse -- By a fountain --

Come, heavy sleep -- Sweet, stay awhile -- Sleep, wayward
thoughts -- Weep you no more, sad fountains -- Fine knacks for
ladies.

493. Dowland, John. Two songs from A pilgrim's solace (1612). Trans.
for voice and piano, with violin obbligato, by Peter Warlock and Philip
Wilson. London: J. & W. Chester, 1923.

Contents: From silent night -- Go nightly cares.

494. An Elizabethan song book: lute songs, madrigals, and rounds.
Music ed. by Noah Greenberg; text ed. by W. H. Auden and Chester
Kallman. New York: Doubleday, 1956.

Contents: Who ever thinks or hopes -- If my complaints -- Can
she excuse my wrongs -- Dear if you change -- Go christall
teares -- His golden locks time -- Come away, come sweet love --
Away with these selfe loving lads -- Come heavy sleepe -- I
saw my lady weepe -- Flow my teares -- Fine knacks for ladies --
O sweet woods -- In darkness let mee dwell -- Weepe you no
more -- The lowest trees have tops.

495. English ayres, Elizabethan and Jacobean. Vol. I-VI. Trans. and
ed. by Peter Warlock and Philip Wilson. London: OUP, 1927-31.

Contents: Vol. I. In darkness let me dwell -- I saw my lady
weep -- Lady, if you so spite me. Vol. III. Time stands
still -- Behold a wonder here. Vol. IV. Lachrimae -- Far from
triumphing court. Vol. V. Sorrow, stay. Vol. VI. Daphne.

496. Fire of love: songs for voice, lute and viola da gamba. Ed. and
trans. by Carl Shavitz. London: Chester Music, 1980.

Contents: Come away, come sweet love.

497. Forty Elizabethan songs. Books I-IV. Ed. and arr. by Edmund
Horace Fellowes. London: Stainer & Bell, 1921-26.

Contents: Book I. Flow my tears -- Say love, if ever thou
didst find. Book II. Sleep wayward thoughts -- Sorrow stay.
Book III. Weep you no more sad fountains -- If my complaints
could passions move -- Awake sweet love. Book IV. I saw my
lady weep -- Fine knacks for ladies.

498. Mirror of love. Ed. and trans. by Carl Shavitz. London:
Chester Music, 197-?

Contents: When Phoebus first did Daphne love.

499. The Oxford choral songs from the old masters. London: OUP,
1923-29.

Contents: Fine knacks for ladies -- By a fountain where I lay.

500. Dowland, Robert. A musicall banquet. Furnished with varietie
of delicious ayres, collected out of the best authors in English,

French, Spanish and Italian ... Printed for Thomas Adams. 1610.

>   Contents: Far from triumphing court -- Lady, if you so spite
>   me -- In darkness let me dwell.

Recordings

501. Dowland, John. The complete works of John Dowland. Editions
de l'Oiseau-lyre, DSLO 508-509, 528-529, 531-532, 517, 551, 553,
585-586, 1976-1981.

>   The Consort of Musicke; Anthony Rooley, conductor; with assisting
>   artists.

502. Dowland, John. The first book of ayres. Dover HCR 5220, 1964.

>   Pro Musica Antiqua of Brussels; Safford Cape, director.
>   Contents: SEE 464.

503. Dowland, John. The first book of ayres. Period Records SPL 727.

>   Pro Musica Antiqua.
>   Contents: SEE 464.

504. Dowland, John. First book of songes, 1597. Editions de
l'Oiseau-lyre DSLO 508-509, 1976.

>   Consort of Musicke; Anthony Rooley, director.
>   Contents: SEE 464.

505. Dowland, John. Second booke of songs, 1600. Editions de
l'Oiseau-lyre DSLO 528-529, 1977.

>   The Consort of Musicke; Anthony Rooley, director.
>   Contents: SEE 470.

506. Dowland, John. Third booke of songs, 1603. Editions de
l'Oiseau-lyre DSLO 531-532, 1977.

>   Consort of Musicke; Anthony Rooley, director.
>   Contents: SEE 474.

507. Dowland, John. A pilgrimes solace, 1612: the fourth booke of
songs. Editions de l'Oiseau-lyre DSLO 585-586, 1981.

>   The Consort of Musicke; Anthony Rooley, director.
>   Contents: SEE 479.

508. Dowland, John. Awake, sweet love: airs and partsongs. Bach
Guild BG 673 (BGS 70673), 1966.

>   Alfred Deller, counter-tenor; Desmond Dupré, lute; Deller Consort.
>   Contents: Wilt thou unkind, thus reave me -- Awake, sweet love --
>   In darkness let me dwell -- Me, me, and none but me -- Go
>   nightly cares -- If my complaints could passions move -- Sleep

wayward thoughts -- Flow not so fast ye fountains -- Come
again -- Sorrow stay -- If that a sinner's sighs -- Fine knacks
for ladies -- Flow my tears -- Can she excuse my wrongs.

509. Dowland, John. Ayres and lute-lessons. Saga 5449, 1977.

James Bowman, counter-tenor; Robert Spencer, lute.
Contents: Come again -- Go, crystal tears -- Can she excuse
my wrongs -- Awake, sweet love -- Sorrow stay -- Shall I sue?
-- Fine knacks for ladies -- What if I never speed? -- Me, me,
and none but me -- Flow not so fast, ye fountains -- When
Phoebus first did Daphne love -- Shall I strive with words to
move? -- Tell me true.

510. Dowland, John. Ayres & lute-lessons. Harmonia Mundi HM 1076,
1982.

Deller Consort.
Contents: What if I never speed -- Go crystal tears -- A shepherd
in a shade -- My thoughts are wing'd with hopes -- Prélude et
gaillarde (lute) -- Rest awhile, you cruel cares -- Tell me
true love -- Wilt thou unkind thus reave me? -- Come again sweet
love doth now invite -- If my complaints should passions move --
Sweet stay awhile -- When Phoebus first did Daphne love -- All
ye whom love or fortune hath betray'd -- Semper Dowland, semper
dolens -- Come heavy sleep -- Away with these self-loving lads.

511. Dowland, John. Ayres for four voices, vol. 1. Westminster Gold
WGM 8246, (195-)

Golden Age Singers; Julian Bream, lute.
Contents: Come again -- Woeful heart -- White as lilies -- If
floods of tears -- Disdain we still -- Sleep, wayward thoughts --
O sweet woods -- Awake sweet love -- Love, these beams that
breed -- When Phoebus first -- Come away, come sweet love -- Dear
if you change -- Shall I sue? -- Come, heavy sleep -- What if I
never speed -- Oh what hath overwrought -- To ask for all thy
love -- Fine knacks for ladies.

512. Dowland, John. Dowland: a miscellany. Editions de l'Oiseau-lyre
DSLO 556, 1979.

John York Skinner, counter-tenor; The Consort of Musicke.
Contents: If my complaints -- Come again -- Sorrow stay.

513. Dowland, John. Dowland songs. Renaissance X27, (19--)

John Langstaff, baritone; Herman Chessid, harpsichord.
Cover title: Purcell-Dowland recital.
Contents: If flood of teares -- Sweet, stay awhile -- Say, love,
if ever thou didst find -- Toss not my soul -- Weep you no more
sad fountains -- When Phoebus first did Daphne love -- Woeful
heart -- I saw my lady weep -- Fine knacks for ladies.

514. Dowland, John. Lute songs. Musical Heritage Society MHS 6825,
(196-)

Russell Oberlin, countertenor; Joseph Iadone, lute.
Contents: Come again -- Thou mighty God -- When David's life --
When the poor cripple -- Can she excuse my wrongs -- Flow not
so fast ye fountains -- I saw my lady weep -- Weep you no more
sad fountains -- Shall I sue? -- Flow my tears -- Far from
triumphing court -- Lady, if you so spite me -- In darkness let
me dwell.

515. Dowland, John. Lute songs. Lyrichord EAS 34, (196-)

Russell Oberlin, countertenor; Joseph Iadone, lute.
Contents: SEE 514.

516. Dowland, John. Lute songs & lute solos. Musical Heritage
Society MHS 1548, 1973.

William Cobb, tenor; Deborah Minkin, lute.
Contents: Flow my teares -- In darkness let me dwell -- Where
sin sore wounding -- Come away, come sweet love -- All ye whom
love or fortune -- Come heavy sleep.

517. Dowland, John. Lute songs, lute solos, consort music. Harmonia
Mundi France HM 244-246, 1978.

Alfred Deller, countertenor; Robert Spencer, lute.
Contents: Flow my tears -- Weep you no more, sad fountains --
Me, me and none but me -- What if I never speed -- Lasso, vita
mia -- Wilt thou, unkind -- Come away, come sweet love -- Sorrow,
stay -- Come again, sweet love -- I saw my lady weep -- Orlando
sleepeth -- From silent night -- If that a sinner's sighs --
Say, love, if ever thou didst find? -- Can she excuse -- If
my complaints could passions move -- Flow not so fast ye fountains
-- Shall I sue? -- In darkness let me dwell -- Can she excuse
my wrongs? -- Come heavy sleep -- Go, nightly cares.

518. Dowland, John. Music of love and friendship. Lyrichord LLST
7153, (197-)

Saltire Singers; Desmond Dupré, lute.
Also released on: Musical Heritage Society MHS 8705, 1968.
Contents: Away with these self-loving lads -- Sweet stay awhile
-- In this trembling shadow -- Now, oh now I needs must part --
What if I never speed -- Me, O me and none but me -- Say love,
if ever thou didst find -- Tell me, true love -- When Phoebus
first did Daphne love -- Think'st thou then by thy feigning --
Where sin sore wounding -- If my complaints could passions move
-- Fine knacks for ladies.

519. Dowland, John. Songs & ayres. Nonesuch H-71167.

Jantina Noorman, soprano; Grayston Burgess, countertenor;
Wilfred Brown, Gerald English, tenors; Christopher Keyte,
bass; and others.
Contents: Where every thought an eye -- An heart that's broken
and contrite -- Shall I sue? -- Go crystal tears -- Love, those
beams that breed -- Say, love, if ever thou didst find -- Welcome,

black night -- Sorrow, stay -- Where sin, sore wounding -- If
that a sinner's sighs -- Lady, if you so spite me -- Weep you
no more sad fountains -- Fine knacks for ladies -- Farewell,
unkind, farewell -- Psalm 51 -- Psalm 100 -- Tell me, true
love -- Up, merry mates.

520. Dowland, John. Songs and dances of John Dowland. Turnabout
TV-S 34510, 1973.

Hugues Cuenod, tenor; Joel Cohen, lute.
Contents: Come away, come sweet love -- Weep you no more --
White as lilies was her face -- Orlando sleepeth -- Awake sweet
love -- Stay, time awhile thy flying -- What if I never speed
-- Fine knacks for ladies -- Come again -- Fortune my foe --
Sorrow stay -- Farewell, unkind -- Now o now -- When Phoebus
first did Daphne love.

521. Dowland, John. Songs of John Dowland. Allegro Classics AL 96,
195-?

DuBose Robertson, tenor; Suzanne Block, lute.
Contents: By a fountain -- Come again -- Can she excuse? --
Me, me, and none but me -- Sorrow stay -- Come away -- Wilt thou
unkind? -- Sleep, wayward thoughts -- Flow, my tears -- Say
love -- Awake sweet love -- Flow not so fast, ye fountain --
What if I never speed? -- If my complaints -- Now, oh now.

522. Dowland, John. Two songs. Archive ARC 3004, 1955.

Renée Soames, tenor; Walter Gerwig, lute; Johannes Kock, viola
da gamba.
Contents: I saw my lady weep -- Flow my tears.

523. Altenglische Lautenlieder. Decca/Serenata 6.41648, 1960.

Title on container: Lute songs - Lautenlieder - Chansons au luth.
Peter Pears, tenor; Julian Bream, lute.
Contents: Sorrow stay -- If my complaints -- What if I never
speed?

524. Ars Britannica: Old Hall Manuscript, madrigals, lute songs.
Telefunken 6.35494, 1980.

Pro Cantione Antiqua.
Contents: A shepherd in a shade -- Fine knacks for ladies --
Where sin sore wounding -- I must complain -- Sweet, stay awhile
-- Now, oh now, I needs must part.

525. Choral music of Poulenc, Vaughan Williams, Holst, Byrd, Dowland.
Lyrichord LLST 7177, 1966.

Schola Cantorum of Oxford.
Contents: What if I never speed.

526. Elizabethan and Jacobean music. Vanguard SRV 306SD, 1971.

Alfred Deller, counter-tenor; Desmond Dupré, lute; Gustav
Leonhardt, harpsichord; Consort of Viols.
Contents: If my complaints could passions move -- Can she excuse
my wrongs -- From silent night.

527. Elizabethan love songs and harpsichord pieces. Lyrichord LLST
737, 1953.

Hugues Cuenod, tenor; Claude Jean Chiasson, harpsichord.
Contents: Weep you no more -- Sorrow stay -- Now, o now, I
needs must part -- Away with these self-loving lads.

528. Elizabethan lute songs. RCA Red Seal LSC-3131, 1970.

Peter Pears, tenor; Julian Bream, lute.
Contents: Can she excuse -- Come heavy sleep -- Dear if you
change -- I saw my lady weep -- Shall I sue? -- Stay time --
Sweet stay awhile -- Weep you no more.

529. Elizabethan lute songs and solos. Philips 6500 282, 1973.

Frank Patterson, tenor; Robert Spencer, lute.
Contents: Fine knacks for ladies -- Shall I sue? -- Away with
these self-loving lads -- In darkness let me dwell -- Come
again: sweet love doth now invite -- What if I never speed --
I saw my lady weep -- Awake, sweet love.

530. Elizabethan serenade. RCA Limited Record Division, 1973.

Previously released as: RCA Victor LSC 2819, 1965.
Peter Pears, tenor; Julian Bream, lute.
Contents: Wilt thou unkind -- Sorrow stay -- The lowest trees
have tops -- Time's eldest son, old age -- In darkness let me
dwell -- Say love, if ever thou didst find.

531. English ayres and duets sung in authentic Elizabethan pronunciation.
Hyperion A66003, 1981.

The Camerata of London.
Contents: Fine knacks for ladies -- In darkness let me dwell --
Time's eldest son, old age -- Flow my tears -- Now, o now, I
needs must part -- Come away, come, sweet love -- Humour, say
what mak'st thou here.

532. English lute songs and six In nomines. Bach Guild BG-576, 1958.

Alfred Deller, counter-tenor; Desmond Dupré, lute.
Contents: What if I never speed -- Shall I sue? -- Come again,
sweet love doth now invite -- Me, me and none but me -- Wilt
thou unkind.

533. English musick for voyces & viols. Titanic Ti 26, 1978.

Jeffrey Gall, countertenor; Frank Hoffmeister, tenor; The New
England Consort of Viols.
Contents: Now, oh now, I needs must part -- Sorrow come.

534. English songs of the 16th and 17th centuries. Abbey LPB712, 1977.

    Gerald English, tenor; David Lumsden, organ/harpsichord; Jane
Ryan, viola da gamba.
Contents: Lady, if you so spite me -- In darkness let me dwell.

535. An evening of Elizabethan verse and its music. Columbia/Odyssey
3216 0171, 1968.

    W.H. Auden; New York Pro Musica Antiqua; Noah Greenberg, director.
Contents: In darkness let me dwell.

536. Frederica von Stade song recital. Columbia M 35127, 1978.

    Contents: Come again -- Sorrow stay.

537. History of music in sound. Vol. 4: The age of humanism. Solo
song. RCA Red Seal LM 6029-2, 1954.

    Various performers.
Contents: Sleep, wayward thoughts.

538. Kissing, drinking and insect songs. Turnabout TV 34485, 1972.

    Sine Nomine Singers.
Contents: It was a time.

539. Late sixteenth century music (Part II). Pleiades Records P256,
1973.

    University of Chicago Collegium Musicum.
Contents: What if I never speed (2 versions).

540. Love songs of the 18th century. Summit SUM 5065, 1978.

    Kurt Equiluz, tenor; Konrad Ragossnig, lute.
Contents: Come again -- Fine knacks for ladies -- If my complaints.

541. Metaphysical tobacco; songs and dances by Dowland, East and
Holborne. Argo ZRG 572, 1968.

    Musica Reservata; Michael Morrow, conductor.
Contents: Sorrow stay -- What if I never speed -- Away with
these self-loving lads -- In this trembling shadow -- Lasso
vita mia -- Welcome black night.

542. Music in Shakespeare's time. Concert Hall CHS 1225, 1954.

    Suzanne Block, accomp. herself on the lute.
Contents: Wilt thou unkind.

543. Music of Shakespeare's time. Oryx EXP 62, 197-?

    Pohlert Renaissance Ensemble.
Contents: What if I never speed -- If my complaints could
passion move -- Flow my tears -- Wilt thou, unkind, thus reave

me? -- Can she excuse my wrongs -- Co crystal tears.

544. <u>O mistress mine; Elizabethan lute songs</u>. Seraphim S-60323, 1979.

James Bowman, countertenor; Robert Spencer, lute.
Contents: Away with these self-loving lads -- Lasso vita mia
-- Now, o now I needs must part -- In darkness let me dwell.

545. <u>O ravishing delight; English songs of the 17th and 18th centuries</u>.
RCA Victrola VICS 1492, 1970.

Also released: Harmonia Mundi DR 215, 197-?
Alfred Deller, counter-tenor; Desmond Dupré, lute and viola
da gamba.
Contents: Shall I sue? -- Come heavy sleep -- I saw my lady
weep -- Wilt thou unkind.

546. <u>A pageant of English song, 1597-1961</u>. EMI/His Master's Voice
HQS 1091, 1967.

Janet Baker, mezzo-soprano; Robert Spencer, lute.
Contents: Come again -- Never love unless you can.

547. <u>Renaissance music</u>. Legend LGD 025, 1977.

Musica Antiqua.
Contents: Flow my tears -- Come again.

548. <u>The Silver swan and other Elizabethan and Jacobean madrigals</u>.
Nonesuch H-71387, 1976.

The Scholars.
Contents: Fine knacks for ladies.

549. <u>Wandering in this place; witty, amourous and introspective ayres
and lute solos of Elizabethan England</u>. 1750 Arch 1757, 1977.

Tom Buckner, voice; Joseph Bacon, lute.
Contents: I saw my lady weep -- Sorrow stay -- If my complaints
could passions move -- Flow not so fast -- Awake, sweet love --
When Phoebus first did Daphne love -- Can she excuse my wrongs.

550. <u>Welcome sweet pleasure; music of England's Golden Age</u>. Columbia
M 35143, 1979.

Waverly Consort; Michael Jaffee.
Contents: Now, oh now, I needs must part.

551. <u>What pleasures have great princes: William Byrd and his con-
temporaries</u>. RCA Red Seal CRL 2-2794, 1977.

The London Early Music Group.
Contents: Can she excuse.

JOHN EARSDEN

Literature

552. Poulton, Diana. "Earsden, John." The new Grove ... London: Macmillan, 1980. V:801.

    Very brief mention of his partnership with George Mason.

Music

553. Earsden, John. The ayres that were sung and played, at Brougham Castle in Westmerland, in the Kings Entertainment: given by the right honourable the Earle of Cumberland, and his right noble sonne the Lord Clifford ... Printed by Thomas Snodham cum. Privelegio. 1618.

    Contents: Tune thy cheerful voice to mine -- Now is the time -- Welcome, welcome, king of guests -- Come follow me my wand'ring mates -- Dido was the Carthage Queen -- Robin is a lovely lad -- The shadows dark'ning our intents -- Truth, sprung from heav'n -- O stay! sweet is the least delay -- Welcome is the word.

554. Earsden, John. The ayres that were sung and played at Brougham Castle, 1618 [by] George Mason and John Earsden. Edited by David Greer. Menston, Eng.: Scolar Press, 1970. 24 p.

    Facsim. of the British Museum copy.
    Series: English lute songs, v. 31.
    Contents: SEE 553.

555. Greaves, Mason and Earsden: Songs (1604) and Ayres (1618). Trans. and ed. by Ian Spink. London: Stainer and Bell; New York: Galaxy Music, 1963. 48 p.

Accomp. ed. from the lute tablature for keyboard instrument.
Series: ELS. Ser. 2, v. 18.
Contents: SEE 553.

ALFONSO FERRABOSCO

Literature

556. Aplin, J. "Sir Henry Fanshawe and two sets of early seventeenth century part books of Christ Church, Oxford." M&L LVII (1976):11-24.

557. Alton, E. H. "The inspired works of Ferrabosco II." RMM III (1970):218.

558. Arkwright, G. E. P. "Alfonso Ferrabosco the younger." In: Studies in music edited by R. Grey. London: Simpkin, Marshall, Hamilton, Kent, 1901. p. 199-214.

559. Arkwright, G. E. P. "Notes on the Ferrabosco family." MA III (1912):220-228; IV (1913):42-54.

560. Brown, David. "William Byrd's 1588 volume." M&L XXXVIII (1957): 372-74.

561. Charteris, Richard. "Matthew Hutton (1638-1711) and his manuscripts in York Minster Library." Galpin SJ XXVIII (April 1975):2-6.

562. Cockshoot, John V. "Ferrabosco, Alfonso (II)." The new Grove ... London: Macmillan, 1980. VI:482-484.

   Includes bibliography.

563. Dart, Thurston. "Jacobean consort music." PRMA LXXXI (1954-55): 63-75.

564. Donington, Robert. "Alfonso Ferrabosco (II)." Grove's dictionary of music and musicians, 5th ed. New York: St. Martin's Press, 1954. III:67-68.

   Short biography, no bibliography.

565. Donington, Robert. "Ferrabosco, Alfonso (II)." MGG IV:49-53.

566. Doughtie, Edward. Lyrics from English airs, 1596-1622. Cambridge, Mass.: Harvard University Press, 1970. 657 p.

567. Duffy, John. The songs and motets of Alfonso Ferrabosco, the younger (1575-1628). Ann Arbor, Mich.: UMI Research Press, 1980. 479 p.

   Includes a biographical introduction and analysis of 38 songs and 14 motets.

568. Duffy, John. The vocal works of Alfonso Ferrabosco, the younger, c. 1575-1628. Diss. Abst. XXXIX (June 1979):7046A

569. "Here and there." Gramophone XXXV (1978):1545.

570. Kerman, Joseph. "Master Alfonso and the English madrigal." MQ XXXVIII (1952):222-44.

571. Livi, Giovanni. "The Ferrabosco family." MA IV (1913):121-142.

572. Peart, D. "Alfonso Ferrabosco and the lyra viol." Musicology II (1965/67):15-21.

573. Vaught, Raymond. The fancies of Alfonso Ferrabosco II. Thesis, Stanford University, 1958. 2 v. Diss. Abst. XIX (May 1959):2975.

574. Vaught, Raymond. "Mersenne's unknown English viol player." Galpin SJ XVII (Feb. 1964):17-23.

575. Warlock, Peter. The English ayre. London: OUP, 1926. 142 p.

   Reprint ed.: Westport, Conn.: Greenwood Press, 1970.
   Chapter 6 is devoted to Alfonso Ferrabosco the younger.

576. Weijers, J. J. "Coperario, Lupo en Ferrabosco, een drietal vergeten Engelse componisten." Mens en Mel XXIII (1968):311-13.

Music

577. Ferrabosco, Alfonso. Ayres ... Printed by T. Snodham, for John Browne, and are to be sould at his shoppe in S. Dunstones Church-yard in Fleetstreet. 1609.

   RISM A/I/3 F256.
   Contents: Like hermit poor -- Come home my troubled thoughts -- Come away, come away -- Dear, when to thee -- Fain I would -- Come, my Celia, let us prove -- So, so, leave off -- Young and simple though I am -- Drown not with tears -- I am a lover -- Why stays the bridegroom? -- Sing we the heroic grace -- With what new thoughts -- Fly from the world -- Shall I seek to ease my grief -- If all these cupids -- So beauty on the waters stood -- Had those that dwell in error -- If all the ages of the earth -- Unconstant love -- O eyes, O mortal stars -- Fair cruel nymph -- What shall I wish -- Tell me, O love.

578. Ferrabosco, Alfonso. <u>Ayres (1609)</u>. Edited by David Greer.
Menston, Eng.: Scolar Press, 1970. 42 p.

    Facsim. of the British Museum copy.
    Series: English lute songs, v. 20.
    Contents: SEE 577.

579. Ferrabosco, Alfonso. <u>Ayres, 1609</u>. Edited by E. H. Fellowes.
London: Stainer & Bell, 1927. 61 p.

    Original accomp. has been trans. from the tablature into modern
    notation for piano; the part for bass instrument has been omitted.
    Series: ESLS. Ser. 2, v. 16.
    Contents: SEE 577.

580. Ferrabosco, Alfonso. <u>Manuscript songs</u>. Trans. and ed. by Ian
Spink. London: Stainer & Bell; New York: Galaxy Music, 1966. 42 p.

    "All but one of these songs are contained in two manuscripts:
    nos. I-IV in the "John Bull" MS 52D, Fitzwilliam Museum,
    Cambridge, and nos. V-XI in MS 1018, St. Michael's College,
    Tenbury. The last song ... is in Egerton MS 2013, British
    Museum."
    Series: ELS. Ser. 2, v. 19.
    Contents: All you forsaken lovers come -- Lo! in a vale there
    sat a shepherdess -- Was I to blame? -- Heav'n, since thou art
    the only place to rest -- Say, shepherd boy -- Nay, nay, you
    must not stay (Ben Jonson's <u>Oberon</u>, 1611) -- Gentle knights
    (<u>Oberon</u>) -- Oh! what a fault (Ben Jonson's <u>Love freed from
    ignorance and folly</u>, 1611) -- Senses by unjust force banish'd
    (<u>Love freed ...</u>) -- How near to good is what is fair (<u>Love
    freed ...</u>) -- Udite! lagrimosi spir'ti d'Averno -- Eterni
    numi -- O crudel' Amarilli -- Lacrimae sempre il mio sommo
    diletto -- Hear me, Oh God!

581. <u>An Elizabethan song book: lute songs, madrigals and rounds</u>.
Music ed. by Noah Greenberg; text ed. by W. H. Auden and Chester
Kallman. New York: Doubleday, 1956.

    Contents: Come my Celia -- So, so leave off this lamenting
    kisse -- So beautie on the waters stood.

582. <u>English ayres, Elizabethan and Jacobean</u>. Vol. I-VI. Trans. and
ed. from the original ed. by Peter Warlock and Philip Wilson. London:
OUP, 1927-31.

    Contents: <u>Vol. II</u>. Shall I seek to ease my grief -- Come, my
    Celia -- Unconstant love -- I am a lover, yet was never loved --
    Fain I would but O I dare not -- O eyes, O moral stars -- Like
    hermit poor -- So, so leave off this last lamenting kiss.

583. <u>Fire of love: songs for voice, lute and viola da gamba</u>. Ed. and
trans. by Carl Shavitz. London: Chester Music, 1980.

    Contents: So beautie on the waters stood.

584. What is love? Ed. and trans. by Carl Shavitz. London: Chester
Music, 197-?

       Contents: Come my Celia.

Recordings

585. English ayres and duets sung in authentic Elizabethan pronunciation.
Hyperion A66003, 1981.

       The Camerata of London.
       Contents: Tell me, O love.

586. An evening of Elizabethan verse and its music. Columbia/Odyssey
3216 0171, 1968.

       W. H. Auden; New York Pro Musica Antiqua; Noah Greenberg, director.
       Contents: Come, my Celia -- So, so, leave off this last lamenting
       kiss.

THOMAS FORD

Literature

587. Aplin, John. "Sir Henry Fanshawe and two sets of early seventeenth-century part books at Christ Church, Oxford." M&L LVII (1976):11-24.

588. Chan, M. "John Hilton's manuscript British Library Add. MS 11608." M&L LX (1979):449ff.

589. Doughtie, Edward. Lyrics from English airs, 1596-1622. Cambridge, Mass.: Harvard University Press, 1970. 657 p.

590. Emden, Cecil S. "Lives of Elizabethan song composers: some new facts." Review of English studies II (1926):416-22.

    Includes "new" biographical information on Ford, Pilkington
    and Peerson.

591. Fortune, Nigel. "Forde, Thomas." MGG IV:508-10.

592. Spink, Ian. "Ford, Thomas." The new Grove ... London: Macmillan, 1980. VI:704-05.

593. Warlock, Peter. The English ayre. London: OUP, 1926. 142 p.

    Reprint ed.: Westport, Conn.: Greenwood Press, 1970.
    Chapter 9 is devoted to Ford and others.

Music

594. Ford, Thomas. Musicke of sundrie kindes, set forth in two bookes. The first whereof are, aires for 4. voices to the lute, orphorion, or

basse-viol, with a dialogue for two voices, and two basse viols in parts, tunde the lute way. The second are pavins, galiards, almaines, toies, jigges, thumpes and such like, for two basse-viols, the liera way, so made as the greatest number may serve to play alone, very easie to be performde ... Imprinted at London by John Windet at the assignes of William Barley and are to be sold by John Browne in Saint Dunstons churchyard in Fleetstreet. 1607.

> RISM A/I/3 F1503.
> Contents: Not full twelve years -- What then is love? -- Unto the temple of thy beauty -- Now I see thy looks were feigned -- Go, passions to the cruel fair -- Come, Phyllis, come to these bowers -- Fair, sweet cruel -- Since first I saw your face -- There is a lady sweet and kind -- How shall I then describe my love? -- Fly not, dear heart.

595. Ford, Thomas. Musicke of sundrie kindes, 1607. Edited by D. Greer. Menston, Eng.: Scolar Press, 1971. 52 p.

> Facsim. of the British Museum copy.
> Series: English lute songs, v. 21.
> Contents: SEE 594.

596. Ford, Thomas. Ten airs from Musicke of Sundrie Kindes (1607). Ed. by E. Fellowes (1921); rev. ed. by T. Dart. London: Stainer and Bell, 1966. 39 p.

> For solo voice and lute; alternative version for voice and piano.
> Series: ELS. Ser. 1, v. 3.
> Contents: SEE 594.

597. Ford, Thomas. "Sigh no more, ladies." Four English songs of the early seventeenth century. Trans. and ed. by Peter Warlock. London: OUP, 1925.

598. An Elizabethan song book: lute songs, madrigals and rounds. Music ed. by Noah Greenberg; text ed. by W. H. Auden and Chester Kallman. New York: Doubleday, 1956.

> Contents: What then is love -- Since first I saw your face -- There is a ladie sweet and kind.

599. Forty Elizabethan songs. Books I-IV. Ed. and arr. by Edmund Horace Fellowes. London: Stainer & Bell, 1921-26.

> Contents: Book I. What then is love, sings Corydon. Book II. Fair sweet cruel. Book III. Now I see thy looks were feigned. Book IV. Not full twelve years twice told -- Come, Phyllis, come to these bowers.

600. The Oxford choral songs from the old masters. London: OUP, 1923-29.

> Contents: There was a lady sweet and kind.

601. What is love? Ed. and trans. by Carl Shavitz. London: Chester Music, 197-?

Contents: What then is love sings Coridon?

Recordings

602.   Altenglische Lautenlieder.   Decca/Serenata 6.41648, 1960.

   Title on slipcase: Lute songs - Lautenlieder - Chansons au luth.
   Peter Pears, tenor; Julian Bream, lute.
   Contents: Come Phyllis come.

603.   Ars Britannica: Old Hall Manuscript, madrigals, lute songs.
Telefunken 6.35494, 1980.

   Pro Cantione Antiqua.
   Contents: Since first I saw -- There is a lady.

604.   Elizabethan lute songs.   RCA Red Seal LSC-3131, (1970)

   Peter Pears, tenor; Julian Bream, lute.
   Contents: Come Phyllis -- Fair sweet cruel.

THOMAS GILES

Literature

605. Pulver, Jeffrey. "Giles, Thomas." A biographical dictionary of old English music. New York: Da Capo Press, 1973. p. 211.

Very brief mention of Thomas Giles.

Music

606. Sabol, Andrew. Four hundred songs and dances from the Stuart masque. Providence, R.I.: Brown University Press, 1978.

Contents: Triumph now with joy and mirth (from Lord Hay's masque)

607. Twenty songs from printed sources. Trans. and ed. by David Greer. London: Stainer and Bell, 1969.

Series: ELS. Ser. 2, v. 21.
Contents: Triumph now with joy and mirth (from Masque in honour of the marriage of Lord Hayes (1607)).

THOMAS GREAVES

Literature

608. Brown, David. "Greaves, Thomas." The new Grove ... London: Macmillan, 1980. VII:656.

609. Doughtie, Edward. Lyrics from English airs, 1596-1622. Cambridge, Mass.: Harvard University Press, 1970. 657 p.

610. Eitner, Robert. "Giulio Abondantes Lautenbücher." MfM VIII (1876):119-21.

611. Fortune, Nigel. "Greaves, Thomas." MGG V:752-53.

612. Husk, William H. and Edmund H. Fellowes. "Thomas Greaves." Grove's dictionary of music and musicians, 5th ed. New York: St. Martin's Press, 1954. III:768.

   Very short biography; no bibliography.

613. Warlock, Peter. The English ayre. London: OUP, 1926. 142 p.

   Reprint ed.: Westport, Conn.: Greenwood Press, 1970.
   Chapter 9 is devoted to Greaves and others.

Music

614. Greaves, Thomas. Songes of sundrie kindes: First, aires to be sung to the lute, and base violl. Next, songes of sadnesse, for the viols and voyce. Lastly, madrigalles, for five voyces ... Imprinted by John Windet dwelling at Powles Wharfe, at the signe of the crosse keyes, and are there to be solde. 1604.

RISM A/I/3 G3718.
Contents: Shaded with olive trees -- Flora, sweet wanton --
Ye bubbling springs -- I will not force my thoughts -- I
prithee sweet John, away -- Nay, will ye faith? -- What is
beauty but a breath -- Stay, Laura, stay! -- Inconstant Laura.

615. Greaves, Thomas. Songs of sundrie kindes, 1604. Ed. by David
Greer. Menston, Eng.: Scolar Press, 1971. 46 p.

Facsim. of the British Museum copy.
Series: English lute songs, v. 22.
Contents: SEE 614.

616. Greaves, Mason, Earsden: songs (1604) and ayres (1618). Trans.
and ed. by Ian Spink. London: Stainer and Bell; New York: Galaxy
Music, 1963. 48 p.

Accomp. ed. from the lute tablature for keyboard instrument.
Series: ELS. Ser. 2, v. 18.
Contents: SEE 614.

617. Greaves, Thomas. "I will not force my thoughts." Trans. and
ed. by Peter Warlock. London; Philadelphia: Curwen, 1926? 5 p.

618. An Elizabethan songbook: lute songs, madrigals, and rounds.
Music ed. by Noah Greenberg; text ed. by W. H. Auden and Chester
Kallman. New York: Doubleday, 1956.

Contents: What is a beauty but a breath.

619. English ayres, Elizabethan and Jacobean. Vol. I-VI. Trans. and
ed. from the original ed. by Peter Warlock and Philip Wilson. London:
OUP, 1927-31.

Contents: Vol. I. Flora. Vol. III. Celestina. Vol. V. What is
beauty but a breath? Vol. VI. Inconstant love.

620. Mirror of love. Ed. and trans. by Carl Shavitz. London:
Chester Music, 197-?

Contents: I pray thee sweet John -- Nay will ye faith.

GEORGE HANDFORD

Literature

621. Doughtie, Edward. "George Handford's ayres: unpublished Jacobean song verse." Anglia LXXXIII (1964):474ff.

622. Doughtie, Edward. "The Handford Book of lute songs (1609)." Forum (Houston) IX (1971):79-80.

623. Doughtie, Edward. Lyrics from English airs, 1596-1622. Cambridge, Mass.: Harvard University Press, 1970. 657 p.

624. Poulton, Diana. "Handford, George." The new Grove ... London: Macmillan, 1980. VIII:140.

Music

625. Handford, George. Ayres to be sunge to ye lute, and base vyole, newly composed by George Handford. (1609).

    Contents: Come sweet fire -- My mournful thoughts -- Florella lay a sleeping -- Two Cynthias did at once appear -- Grief press my soul -- Go weep sad soul -- Groan weary soul -- If the tongue durst oneword speak -- Come sullen night -- Say ye gods that powers have -- Hide not from me those eyes -- Now each creature joyes the other -- You watry issue of a mourning mind -- Breath out my sighs -- Flow flow my teares -- Come teares and sighs -- Ah now I fall -- But now I rise -- See o see Amyntas -- Daphny stay o stay.

626. Handford, George. Ayres to be sunge to the lute (ca. 1609). Ed. by David Greer. Menston, Eng.: Scolar Press, 1970. 56 p.

Facsim. of MS.R.16.29 in the library of Trinity College,
Cambridge.
Series: English lute songs, v. 23.
Contents: SEE 625.

627. English ayres, Elizabethan and Jacobean. Vol. I-VI. Trans. and
ed. from the original ed. by Peter Warlock and Philip Wilson. London:
OUP, 1927-31.

Contents: Vol. VI. Go weep, sad soul.

628. Fire of love: songs for voice, lute and viola da gamba. Ed. and
trans. by Carl Shavitz. London: Chester Music, 1980.

Contents: Come, come sweet fire.

TOBIAS HUME

Literature

629. Bent, Margaret. "Hume, Tobias." The new Grove ... London: Macmillan, 1980. VIII:776.

630. Doughtie, Edward. Lyrics from English airs, 1596-1622. Cambridge, Mass.: Harvard University Press, 1970. 657 p.

631. Fortune, Nigel. "Hume, Tobias." MGG VI:918-19.

632. Harris, C. A study and partial transcription of 'The first part of ayres' by Tobias Hume. Thesis, University of London, 1971.

633. Harris, C. "Tobias Hume--a short biography." Chelys III (1971):16ff.

634. Hume, Tobias. The first part of ayres (1605). Captaine Humes poeticall musicke (1607). Hrsg. von/ed. by Sterling Jones, mit einer Einleitung von/with an introduction by Veronika Gutmann. Winterthur, Switz.: Amadeus, 1980.

   The introduction comments on Hume's life and works; instrumentation and performance suggestions.

635. Husk, William H. "Tobias Hume." Grove's dictionary of music and musicians, 5th ed. New York: St. Martin's Press, 1954. IV:404.

   Very brief biography; no bibliography.

636. Sullivan, W. Tobias Hume's 'First part of ayres' 1605. Thesis, University of Hawaii, 1967.

   Serialized in Journal of the Viola da Gamba Society of America V (1968)-IX (1972).

637. Warlock, Peter. The English ayre. London: OUP, 1926. 142 p.

Reprint ed.: Westport, Conn.: Greenwood Press, 1970.
Chapter 5 is devoted to Captain Tobias Hume.

Music

638. Hume, Tobias. Captaine Humes poeticall musicke. Principally
made for two basse-viols, yet so construied, that it may be plaied
8. severall waies upon sundry instruments with much facilitie. I.
The first way or musicke is for one bass-viole to play alone in parts,
which standeth alwaies on the right side of the booke. 2. The second
musicke is for two basse-viols to play together. 3. The third musicke,
for three basse-viols to play together. 4. The fourth musicke, for
two tenor viols and a basse-viole. 5. Fift musicke, for two lutes and
a basse-viole. 6. The sixt musicke, for two orpherions and a basse-
viole. 7. The seventh musicke, to use the voyce to some of these
musicks, but especially to the three basse-viols, or to the two
orpherions with one basse-viole to play the ground. 8. The eight
and last musicke, is consorting all these instruments together with
the virginals, or rather with a winde instrument and the voice ...
Printed by John Windet, 1607.

RISM A/I/4 H7886.
Contents: Cease, leaden slumber, dreaming -- What greater grief
-- Come, come my heart.

639. Hume, Tobias. Poeticall musicke (1607). Ed. by Frank
Traficante. Menston, Eng.: Scolar Press, 1969. 57 p.

Facsim. of the British Museum copy.
Series: English lute songs, v. 25.
Contents: SEE 638.

640. Hume, Tobias. The first part of ayres, French, Pollish and
others together, some in tabliture, and some in pricke-song: with
pavines, galliards, and almaines for the viole de gambo alone, and
other musicall conceits for two base viols, expressing five partes,
with pleasant reportes one from the other, and for two leero viols,
and also for the leero viole with two treble viols, or two with one
treble. Lastly, for the leero viole to play alone, and some songes to
bee sung to the viole, with the lute, or better with the viole alone.
Also, an invention for two to play upon one viole ... Printed by John
Windet, dwelling at the signe of the crosse keyes at Powles Wharfe.
1605.

RISM A/I/4 H7885.
Contents: What greater grief -- Fainewould I change that note --
Tobacco! Tobacco! -- The soldier's song.

641. Hume, Tobias. The first part of ayres (1605). Ed. by Frank
Traficante. London: Scolar Press, 1969. 69 p.

Facsim. of the British Museum copy.
Series: English lute songs, v. 24.
Contents: SEE 640.

642. Hume, Tobias. The first part of ayres (1605); Captaine Humes
poeticall musicke (1607). Hrsg. von/ed. by Sterling Jones. Mit
einer Einleitung von/with an introduction by Veronika Gutmann.
Winterthur, Switz.: Amadeus, 1980. 271 p.

Introduction in German and English.
Contents: The first part of ayres (1605). The souldier's
song -- Tobacco -- Alas poore men -- What greater grief.
Captaine Humes poeticall musicke (1607). The queenes New-
yeares gift (Cease leaden slumber) -- What greater grief --
The hunting song.

643. An Elizabethan songbook: lute songs, madrigals, and rounds.
Music ed. by Noah Greenberg; text ed. by W. H. Auden and Chester
Kallman. New York: Doubleday, 1956.

Contents: Tobacco is like love -- Fain would I change that note.

644. English ayres, Elizabethan and Jacobean. Vol. I-VI. Trans. and
ed. from the original ed. by Peter Warlock and Philip Wilson. London:
OUP, 1927-31.

Contents: Vol. III. Tobacco. Vol. IV. Fain would I change that
note.

645. Forty Elizabethan songs. Book I-IV. Ed. and arr. with original
accomp. by Edmund Horace Fellowes. London: Stainer & Bell, 1921-26.

Contents: Book III. Fain would I change that note.

646. The Oxford choral songs from the old masters. London: OUP,
1923-29.

Contents: Fain would I change that note.

Recordings

647. Character songs (by various composers). Editions de l'Oiseau-
lyre DSLO 545, 1980.

The Consort of Musicke; Anthony Rooley, conductor.
Contents: Tobacco, tobacco.

648. English ayres and duets sung in authentic Elizabethan pronunciation.
Hyperion A66003, 1981.

Contents: Tobacco, tobacco.

ROBERT JOHNSON

Literature

649. Arkwright, G. E. P. "Robert Johnson." Grove's dictionary of music and musicians, 5th ed. New York: St. Martin's Press, 1954. IV:649-50.

Short biography; no bibliography.

650. Boetticher, Wolfgang and David Lumsden. "Johnson, Robert." MGG VII:133-35.

651. Chan, M. "John Hilton's manuscript British Museum Library Add. MS 11608." M&L LX (1979):449ff.

652. Covell, R. "Seventeenth century music for 'The Tempest.'" Studies Mus II (1968):45-64.

653. Cutts, John P. The contribution of Robert Johnson, King's Musician to Court and Theatrical Entertainments, and the tradition of such service prior to 1642. Unpubl. Ph.D. diss., University of Reading (England), 1955.

654. Cutts, John P. "Robert Johnson and the court masque." M&L XLI (1960):111-26.

655. Cutts, John P. "Robert Johnson: King's musician in his majesty's public entertainment." M&L XXXVI (1955):110-25.

656. Fiske, R. "The 'MacBeth' music." M&L XLV (1964):114-25.

657. Flood, William H. "New light on late Tudor composers--Robert Johnson." MT LXVI (1925):904-05.

658. Fuller, David. "The Jonsonian masque and its music." M&L
LIV (1973):440ff.

659. Holman, P. "The Jonsonian masque." M&L LV (1974):250ff.

660. Jeffery, Brian. "The lute music of Robert Johnson." EM
II (1974):105-09.

661. Lumsden, David, Ian Spink and P. Holman. "Johnson, Robert."
The new Grove ... London: Macmillan, 1980. IX:681-82.

    Includes a full list of his compositions.

662. Moore, R. E. "The music to 'MacBeth'." MQ XLVII (1981):22-40.

663. Nagel, Wilibald. "Annalen der englischen Hofmusik von der Zeit
Heinrichs VIII bis zum Tode Karl I (1509-1649)." Beilage MfM XXVI
(1894):40-42.

<u>Music</u>

664. Johnson, Robert. Ayres, songs and dialogues. Trans. and ed.
by Ian Spink. London: Stainer & Bell; New York: Galaxy Music, 1961.
75 p.

    Accomp. ed. from the lute tablature for keyboard instrument.
    Series: ELS. Ser. 2, v. 17.
    Contents: Miscellaneous ayres. As I walk'd forth -- Come heavy
    sleep -- Dear, do not you fair beauty wrong -- With endless
    tears -- For ever let thy heav'nly tapers -- Shall I like a
    hermit dwell? -- Woods, rocks, and mountains -- How wretched is
    the state.
    Songs from plays. Arm, arm! (Beaumont and Fletcher, The mad lover,
    c. 1616) -- Full fathom five (Shakespeare, The Tempest, 1611) --
    Where the bee sucks (The Tempest) -- Away delights (Beaumont and
    Fletcher, The Captain, c. 1612) -- Come hither you that love
    (The Captain) -- Oh, let us howl (Webster, The dutchess of Malfi,
    c. 1613) -- Care charming sleep (Beaumont and Fletcher,
    Valentinian, c. 1614) -- Come away, thou lady gay! (Beaumont and
    Fletcher, The chances, c. 1617) -- From the famous Peak of Derby
    (Jonson, The gypsies metamorphosed, 1621) -- 'Tis late and cold
    (Beaumont and Fletcher, The lover's progress, 1623) -- Charon, oh
    Charon (dialogue).
    Songs attributed to Johnson. Hark, hark! the lark (Shakespeare,
    Cymbelene, c. 1609) -- Adieu, fond love (Beaumont and Fletcher,
    The lover's progress, 1623) -- Come away, Hecate! (Middleton,
    The witch, c. 1616) -- Get you hence, for I must go (Shakespeare,
    A winter's tale, c. 1611) -- Have you seen the bright lily grow?
    (Jonson, The devil is an ass, 1616) -- Orpheus I am (Beaumont and
    Fletcher, The mad lover, c. 1616) -- Tell me, dearest (Beaumont
    and Fletcher, The Captain, c. 1612)

665. Johnson, Robert. Ayres, songs and dialogues. Trans. and ed.
by Ian Spink. 2d rev. ed. London: Stainer & Bell; New York: Galaxy

Music, 1974.   80 p.

    Rev. ed.
    Accomp. ed. from the lute tablature for keyboard instrument.
    Series: ELS. Ser. 2, v. 17.
    Contents: SEE 664.

666. Sabol, Andrew J. Four hundred songs and dances from the Stuart
masque. Providence, R.I.: Brown University Press, 1978.

    Contents: From the famous Peak of Derby (The gypsie's song).

667. Johnson, Robert. William Shakespeare, two songs from 'The tempest'
set by his contemporary Robert Johnson, together with two other songs
by the same composer. Ed. by Anthony Lewis. Paris: Lyrebird Press,
1936. 18 p.

    For solo voice with piano accomp.
    Contents: Full fathom five -- Where the bee sucks -- Care charming
    sleep -- Mine host's song.

Recordings

668. English lute songs and six In nomines. Bach Guild BG 576, 1958.

    Alfred Deller, counter-tenor; Desmond Dupré, lute.
    Contents: Care charming sleep (Valetinian).

669. Masque music: instrumental and vocal music from the Stuart
masque. Nonesuch H 71153, 1967.

    Concentus Musicus of Denmark; Aksel Mathlesen, conductor.
    Contents: The fairy masque -- The satyr's masque -- The gypsies'
    masque.

670. Music für Kaiser, König, Bettelmann. RCA RL 25140, 1978.

    Paul Elliott, tenor; Geoffrey Shaw, baritone; The London Early
    Music Group.
    Contents: The satyres masque.

671. O mistress mine; Elizabethan lute songs. Seraphim S-60323, 1979.

    James Bowman, countertenor; Robert Spencer, lute.
    Contents: Full fathoms five -- Where the bee sucks.

672. What pleasures have great princes; William Byrd and his
contemporaries. RCA Red Seal CRL 2-2794, 1977.

    The London Early Music Group.
    Contents: Satyres masque.

ROBERT JONES

Literature

673. Adams, Joseph Q. "A new song by Robert Jones." <u>MLQ</u> I (1940): 45-48.

      Facsim. of manuscript with biographical note.

674. Brown, David. "Jones, Robert." <u>The new Grove ...</u> London: Macmillan, 1980. IX:703-04.

      Includes bibliography.

675. Cutts, John P. "Everie woman in her humor." <u>RenaisN</u> VIII (1965): 123-26.

676. Cutts, John P. "A reconsideration of the 'Willow song'." <u>JAMS</u> X (1957):14-24.

677. Doughtie, Edward. <u>Lyrics from English airs, 1596-1622</u>. Cambridge, Mass.: Harvard University Press, 1970. 657 p.

678. Fellowes, Edmund H. "Robert Jones." <u>Grove's dictionary of music and musicians, 5th ed</u>. New York: St. Martin's Press, 1954. IV:660-61.

      Jones is discussed as a composer of ayres and madrigals.

679. Fellowes, Edmund H. "The texts of the song books of Robert Jones." <u>M&L</u> VIII (1927):25-37.

680. Flood, William H. "New light on the late Tudor composers-- XXXV. Robert Jones." <u>MT</u> LXIX (1928):616-17.

681. Fortune, Nigel. "Jones, Robert." <u>MGG</u> VII:162-64.

682. Greer, David. "'What if a day'--an examination of the words and music." M&L XLIII (1962):304-19.

683. Mies, Otto H. "Elizabethan music prints in an East Prussian castle." MD III (1949):171-72.

Briefly notes rare copies of early editions of works by John and Robert Dowland and Robert Jones.

684. Pattison, K. An analysis of the ayres of Robert Jones. Unpubl. thesis (M.F.A.), University of Georgia, 1965. 86 p.

685. Warlock, Peter. The English ayre. London: OUP, 1926. 142 p.

Reprint ed.: Westport, Conn.: Greenwood Press, 1970.
Chapter 4 is devoted to Robert Jones.

686. Warlock, Peter. "Robert Jones and his prefaces." MT LXIV (1923):99ff.

Music

687. Jones, Robert. The first booke of songes & ayres of foure parts with tableture for the lute. So made that all the parts together, or either of them severally may be song to the lute, orpherian or viol de gambo ... Printed by Peter Short with the assent of Thomas Morley, and are to be sold at the signe of the starre on Bredstreet Hill. 1600.

RISM A/I/4 J642.
Contents: A woman's looks -- Fond wanton youths -- She whose matchless beauty -- Once did I love -- Led by a strong desire -- Lie down, poor heart -- Where lingering fear -- Hero, care not though they pry -- When love on time and measure -- Sweet, come away, my darling -- Women, what are they? -- Farewell, dear love -- O my poor eyes -- If fathers knew but how to leave -- Life is a poet's fable -- Sweet Philomel in groves and deserts -- That heart, wherein all sorrows -- What if I seek for love of thee -- My mistress sings no other song -- Perplexed sore am I -- Can modest plain desire.

688. Jones, Robert. The first book of songes or ayre, 1600. Ed. by David Greer. Menston, Eng.: Scolar Press, 1970. 51 p.

Facsim. ed.: Reproduced from copies in the British Museum and the Folger Shakespeare Library.
Series: English lute songs, v. 26.
Contents: SEE 687.

689. Jones, Robert. The first booke of songes and ayres (1600). London: Stainer & Bell, 1925. 43 p.

Trans., scored and ed. by Edmund H. Fellowes.
Series: ESLS. Ser. 2, v. 4.
Contents: SEE 687.

690. Jones, Robert. The first booke of songes and ayres (1600). Ed.
by Edmund H. Fellowes; rev. by Thurston Dart. London: Stainer &
Bell, 1959. 43 p.

>   Rev. ed.; for voice and piano.
>   Series: ELS. Ser. 2, v. 4.
>   Contents: SEE 687.

691. Jones, Robert. The second booke of songs and ayres, set out
to the lute, the base violl the playne way, or the base by tableture
after the leero fashion ... Printed by P.S. for Mathew Selman by the
assent of Thomas Morley, and are to be sold at the inner temple gate.
1601.

>   RISM A/I/4 J643.
>   Contents: Love winged my hopes -- My love bound me with a kiss --
>   O my thoughts do beat me -- Dreams and imaginations -- Methought
>   this other night -- Whoso is tied -- Fie, what a coil is here --
>   Beauty, stand further -- Now what is love -- Love's god is a boy
>   -- Over these brooks -- Whither runneth my sweet heart? -- Once
>   did I love -- Fair women like fair jewels are -- Dainty darling
>   kind and free -- My love is neither young nor old -- Love is a
>   bable -- Arise, my thoughts -- Did ever man thus love -- To
>   sigh and to be sad -- Come, sorrows, come.

692. Jones, Robert. The second booke of songs and ayres 1601. Ed.
by David Greer. Menston, Eng.: Scolar Press, 1971. 51 p.

>   Facsim. ed. of the British Museum copy.
>   Series: English lute songs, v. 27.
>   Contents: SEE 691.

693. Jones, Robert. Second booke of ayres (1601). Trans., scored
and ed. by E. H. Fellowes. London: Stainer & Bell, 1926. 53 p.

>   For solo voice with lute accomp. trans. from the tablature
>   into modern notation for piano.
>   Series: ESLS. Ser. 2, v. 5.
>   Contents: SEE 691.

694. Jones, Robert. Ultimum vale, with a triplicity of musicke,
whereof the first part is for the lute, the voyce, and the viole
degambo. The 2. part for the lute, the viole, and foure partes to sing.
The third part is for two trebles, to sing either to the lute, or the
viole or to both, if any please ... Printed at London by John Windet
and are to be sold by Simon Waterson, in Powles Churchyard, at the
signe of the crowne. 1605.

>   RISM A/I/4 J644.
>   Contents: Do not, O do not prize -- Beauty sat bathing by a
>   spring -- Go to bed, sweet muse -- Shall I look to ease my
>   grief -- What if I sped -- Sweet, if you like -- Cease, troubled
>   thoughts -- Cynthia, queen of seas and lands -- Blame not my
>   cheeks -- There is a garden in her face -- Sweet love, my only
>   treasure -- Think'st thou, Kate, to put me down? -- When will
>   the fountains of my tears? -- Fly from the world -- Happy he --

Disdain that so doth fill me -- Now let her change -- Since
first disdain began to rise -- At her fair hands -- Oft have I
mused -- Now have I learned with much ado.

695. Jones, Robert. Ultimum vale, or The third booke of ayres, 1605.
Ed. by David Greer. Menston, Eng.: Scolar Press, 1971. 51 p.

Facsim. of copy in the Royal College of Music, London.
Series: English lute songs, v. 28.
Contents: SEE 694.

696. Jones, Robert. Ultimum vale, third booke of ayres (1608). Trans.,
scored and ed. from original ed. by E. H. Fellowes. London: Stainer &
Bell, 1926. 57 p.

Original lute accomp. has been trans. from the tablature into
modern notation for the piano.
Series: ESLS. Ser. 2, v. 6.
Contents: SEE 694.

697. Jones, Robert. A musicall dreame. Or the fourth booke of ayres,
the first part is for lute, two voyces, and the viole de gambo; the
second part is for the lute, the viole and foure voices to sing; the
third part is for one voyce alone, or to the lute, the basse viole, or
to both if you please, whereof, two are Italian ayres ..1 Imprinted by
the assignes of William Barley, and are to be solde in Powles Churchyeard, at the signe of the crowne. 1609.

RISM A/I/4 J646.
Contents: Though your strangeness -- Sweet Kate -- Once did I
serve a cruel heart -- Will said to his mammy -- Hark! wot ye
what? -- My complaining is but feigning -- On a time in summer
season -- Farewell, fond youth -- How should I show my love?
O he is gone -- And is it night? -- She hath an eye -- I know
not what -- Grief of my best love's absenting -- If in this
flesh -- O thread of life -- When I sit reading -- Fain would
I speak -- In Sherwood lived stout Robin Hood -- Ite, caldi
sospiri -- S'amor non è.

698. Jones, Robert. A musicall dreame (1609). Ed. by David Greer.
Menston, Eng.: Scolar Press, 1967. 52 p.

Facsim. of copy in the Huntington Library.
Series: English lute songs, v. 29.
Contents: SEE 697.

699. Jones, Robert. A musicall dreame or, Fourth booke of ayres, 1609.
Trans., scored and ed. from the original ed. by E. H. Fellowes.
London: Stainer & Bell, 1927. 62 p.

Original lute accomp. trans. from the tablature into modern
notation for the piano.
Series: ESLS. Ser. 2, v. 14.
Contents: SEE 697.

700. Jones, Robert. <u>The muses gardin for delights, or The fift
booke of ayres, onely for the lute, the base-vyoll, and the voyce</u> ...
Printed by the assignes of William Barley. 1610.

> RISM A/I/4 J647.
> Contents: Love is a pretty frenzy -- Soft, Cupid, soft! -- As
> I the seely fish deceive -- The fountains smoke -- Walking by
> the river side -- I cannot choose but give a smile -- Joy in
> thy hope -- How many new years -- There was a shepherd -- The
> sea hath many thousand sands -- Once did my thoughts -- I am
> so far from pitying thee -- As I lay lately in a dream -- There
> was a wily lad -- My father fain would have me take -- My love
> hath her true love betrayed -- All my sence thy strangeness
> gained -- To thee, deaf asp -- Behold her locks -- Although the
> wings of my desires -- Might I redeem mine errors.

701. Jones, Robert. <u>The muses gardin, or The fifth booke of ayres,
London, 1610</u>. Ed. by David Greer. Menston, Eng.: Scolar Press, 1970.
35 p.

> Facsim. of the copy in the Huntington Library.
> Series: English lute songs, v. 30.
> Contents: SEE 700.

702. Jones, Robert. <u>The muses gardin for delights; or Fifth booke
of ayres, 1610</u>. Trans., scored and ed. from the original ed. by
E. H. Fellowes. London: Stainer & Bell, 1927. 53 p.

> Original accomp. trans. from the tablature into modern notation
> for piano.
> Series: ESLS. Ser. 2, v. 15.
> Contents: SEE 700.

703. <u>An Elizabethan song book: lute songs, madrigals, and rounds</u>.
Music ed. by Noah Greenberg; text ed. by W. H. Auden and Chester
Kallman. New York: Doubleday, 1956.

> Contents: When love on time and measure makes his ground --
> Dreames and imaginations -- Now what is love -- Beauty sate
> bathing -- Go to bed sweete muze -- Love is a bable -- What if
> I sped -- Sweet if you like and love me stil -- Sweete Kate --
> Will saide to his mammy -- In Sherwood livde stout Robin Hood --
> Ite caldi sospiri -- There was a wyly ladde.

704. <u>English ayres, Elizabethan and Jacobean</u>. Vol. I-VI. Trans.
and ed. from the original ed. by Peter Warlock and Philip Wilson.
London: OUP, 1927-31.

> Contents: <u>Vol. I</u>. Love's god is a boy -- Now what is love --
> Did ever man thus love as I -- My love is neither young nor
> old -- Sweet if you like and love me still -- Go to bed, sweet
> muse. <u>Vol. II</u>. Love is a pretty frenzy -- Soft, Cupid, soft --
> As I the silly fish deceive -- Walking by a river side -- Joy
> in thy hope -- There is a shepherd that did live -- The sea
> hath many thousand sands -- Once did my thoughts both ebb and
> flow -- I am so far from pitying thee -- There was a wily lad --

My father fain would have me take -- All my sense thy sweetness
gained. <u>Vol. III</u>. What if I sped where I least expected -- My
love bound me with a kiss -- Fair women like fair jewels are --
Beauty sat bathing by a spring -- Dreams and imaginations -- Fie,
what a coil is here. <u>Vol. IV</u>. In Sherwood lived stout Robin
Hood -- Do not, O do not prize -- Sweet Kate. <u>Vol. V</u>. Shall I
look to ease my grief? -- Beauty, stand further -- Whither
runneth my sweet heart? <u>Vol. VI</u>. Whoso is tied -- Oh, how do my
thought do beat me -- My complain is but feigning.

705. <u>Fire of love: songs for voice, lute and viola da gamba</u>. Ed.
and trans. by Carl Shavitz. London: Chester Music, 1980.

Contents: My love is neither young nor old.

706. <u>Forty Elizabethan songs</u>. Books I-IV. Ed. and arr. with the
original accomp. by Edmund Horace Fellowes. London: Stainer & Bell,
1921-26.

Contents: <u>Book I</u>. In Sherwood lived stout Robin Hood. <u>Book II</u>.
Now what is love? <u>Book III</u>. Love is a bable. <u>Book IV</u>. Love's
god is a boy.

707. <u>Mirror of love</u>. Ed. and trans. by Carl Shavitz. London:
Chester Music, 197-?

Contents: My thoughts this other night -- My mistress sings
no other song -- Sweet Philomell.

708. <u>The Oxford choral songs from the old masters</u>. London: OUP,
1923-29.

Contents: In Sherwood lived stout Robin Hood -- Do not, o do
not -- Sweet Kate.

709. <u>What is love?</u> Ed. and trans. by Carl Shavitz. London: Chester
Music, 197-?

Contents: Love is a bable -- Love is a prettie frencie -- Now
what is love I pray thee tell.

Recordings

710. <u>Ars Britannica: Old Hall Manuscript, madrigals, lute songs</u>.
Telefunken 6.35494, 1980.

Pro Cantione Antiqua.
Contents: Thinkst thou Kate.

711. <u>Elizabethan ayres and duets sung in authentic Elizabethan
pronunciation</u>. Hyperion A66003, 1981.

The Camerata of London.
Contents: Now what is love?

712. <u>Elizabethan love songs and harpsichord pieces</u>. Lyrichord LLST 737, 1953.

>   Hughes Cuenod, tenor; Claude Jean Chiasson, harpsichord.
>   Contents: Go to bed, sweet muse -- Sweet Kate.

713. <u>An evening of Elizabethan verse and its music</u>. Columbia/Odyssey 3216 0171, 1968.

>   W.H. Auden; New York Pro Musica Antiqua; Noah Greenberg, director.
>   Contents: Sweet if you like and love me still -- Sweet Kate of late -- Though your strangeness.

714. <u>Music for voices and viols in the time of Shakespeare</u>. ABC Records WGS 8216, 1973.

>   Golden Age Singers; Elizabethan Consort, viols; Herman Leeb, lute.
>   Contents: Farewell, my dear.

715. <u>Music in Shakespeare's time</u>. Concert Hall CHS 1225, 1954.

>   Suzanne Block, accomp. herself on the lute.
>   Contents: Farewell, dear love.

716. <u>Musik für Kaiser, König, Bettelmann</u>. RCA RL 25140, 1978.

>   Paul Elliott, tenor; Geoffrey Shaw, baritone; The London Early Music Group.
>   Contents: To sigh and to bee sad -- Whither runneth my sweet hart.

717. <u>A Russell Oberlin recital</u>. Decca DL 10032, (1961).

>   Russell Oberlin, countertenor with various accompaniments.
>   Contents: Love is a bable -- Ite caldi sospri -- As I lay lately in a dream -- Go to bed sweet muze.

718. <u>Top hits, c. 1420-1635 A.D.</u> Project 3 Total Sound PR7000SD, 1967.

>   Renaissance Quartet.
>   Contents: Farewell, dear love.

719. <u>What pleasures have great princes: William Byrd and his contemporaries</u>. RCA Red Seal CRL 2-2794, 1977.

>   The London Early Music Group.
>   Contents: To sigh and to bee sad -- Whither runneth my sweet heart.

NICHOLAS LANIER

Literature

720. Chan, M. "John Hilton's manuscript British Library Add. MS 11608." M&L LX (1979):449ff.

721. Charteris, Richard. "Jacobean musicians at Hatfield House, 1605-1613." RMA XII (1974):115-36.

722. Cust, L. "The Lanier family." Miscellanea genealogica et heraldica, 5th ser., VI (1926-28):375ff.

723. Duckles, Vincent. "English song and the challenge of Italian monody." In: V. Duckles and F.B. Zimmerman. Words to music. Los Angeles: University of California, 1967. p. 3-42.

724. Emslie, McDonald. "Nicholas Lanier's innovations in English song." M&L XLI (1960):13-27.

725. Fuller-Maitland, J. A. "Nicholas Lanier." Grove's dictionary of music and musicians, 5th ed. New York: St. Martin's Press, 1954. V:51.

    Lanier is briefly discussed as a singer, composer and painter.

726. Graham, F. L. The earlier life and work of Nicholas Lanier ... collector of paintings and drawings. Diss., Columbia University, 1967.

727. Sabol, Andrew J. "Introduction" (to) A score for 'Lovers made men': a masque by Ben Jonson. Providence, R.I.: Brown University Press, 1963.

728. Sabol, Andrew J. Songs and dances for the Stuart masque. Providence, R.I.: Brown University Press, 1959. 172 p.

"An edition of 63 items of music for the English court masque
from 1604 to 1641, with an introductory essay."
1978 ed.: Four hundred songs and dances for the Stuart masque.

729. Smallman, B. "Endor revisited: English biblical dialogues of
the seventeenth century." M&L XLVI (1965):137ff.

730. Spink, Ian. "English cavalier songs, 1620-1660." PRMA LXXXVI
(1959):61-78.

731. Spink, Ian. "Lanier, Nicholas." The new Grove ... London:
Macmillan, 1980. X:454-55.

Includes a list of his works.

732. Spink, Ian. "Lanier in Italy." M&L XL (1959):242-52.

733. Sternfeld, Frederick W. Music in Shakespearean tragedy. London:
Routledge and Kegan Paul, 1963. 333 p.

2d ed.: London: Routledge, 1967. 334 p.

Music

Stage works: Maske ... at the marriage of ... the Earle of
Somerset (Campion, collab. with G. Coprario) -- Lovers made men
(Jonson) -- The vision of delight (Jonson) -- The gypsies metamorphosed
(Jonson, collab. with R. Johnson) -- The masque of Augurs (Jonson,
collab. with A. Ferrabosco).

Surviving vocal works: Bring away this sacred tree -- Colin
say why sit'st thou so -- Come, thou glorious object of my sight --
Do not expect to hear of all thy good -- Fire, lo here I burn -- I
prithee keep my sheep for me -- I was not wearier when I lay -- I
wish no more thou should'st love me -- In guilty night -- Like hermit
poor -- Love and I of late did part -- Mark how the blushful morn --
Neither sighs, nor tears, nor mourning -- No, I tell thee, no --
No more shall meads -- Nor com'st thou yet -- Of thee, kind boy --
Shepherd, in faith, I cannot stay -- Silly heart, forbear -- Stay,
silly heart, and do not break -- Sweet do not thus destroy me --
Tell me shepherd, dost thou love -- Thou art not fair -- Thou I am
young -- Weep no more my wearied eyes -- White thou ye be -- Young and
simple though I am -- Amorosa pargoletta -- Miser pastorella -- Qual
musico gentil.

734. Lanier, Nicholas. Six songs. Ed. by E. H. Jones. London:
Galliard; New York: Galaxy Music, 1976. 15 p.

For voice and continuo; figured bass realized for keyboard
instrument.
Contents: Like hermit poor -- Though I am young -- Come, come
thou glorious object -- Thou art not fair -- Young and simple
though I am -- Mark how the blushful morn.

735. English songs, 1625-1660. Ed. by Ian Spink. London: OUP, 1971.

Series: Musica britannica, v. 33.

736. Playford, John, publisher. Select ayres and dialogues for one, two, and three voyces, to the theorbo-lute or basse-viol. Composed by John Wilson, Charles Colman, Henry Lawes, William Lawes, Nicholas Laneare, William Webb, and other excellent masters of musicke. London: Printed by W. Godbid for John Playford ... 1659.

Contents: I prethee keep my sheep for me -- No beauty without me.

737. Sabol, Andrew J. Four hundred songs and dances from the Stuart masque. Providence, R.I.: Brown University Press, 1978.

Contents: Bring away this sacred tree -- I was not wearier -- Do not expect to hear of all.

738. A score for 'Lovers made men'. Ed. by Andrew J. Sabol. Providence, R.I.: Brown University Press, 1963. 93 p.

Includes pieces by Lanier.

739. Twenty songs from printed sources. Trans. and ed. by David Greer. London: Stainer & Bell, 1969.

Contents: Bring away this sacred tree.

GEORGE MASON

Literature

740. Fellowes, Edmund H. "George Mason." Grove's dictionary of
music and musicians, 5th ed. New York: St. Martin's Press, 1954. V:611.

 Brief mention of George Mason.

741. Poulton, Diana. "Mason, George." The new Grove ... London:
Macmillan, 1980. XI:752.

 Short biography.

Music

742. Mason, George and John Earsden. The ayres that were sung and
played at Brougham Castle in Westmerland, in the kings entertainment:
given the right honourable the Earle of Cumberland, and his right
noble sonne the Lord Clifford ... Printed by Thomas Snodham cum.
privelegio. 1618.

 RISM A/I/5 M1256.
 Contents: Tune thy cheerful voice to mine -- Now is the time --
 Welcome, welcome, king of guests -- Come follow me my wand'ring
 mates -- Dido was the Carthage Queen -- Robin is a lovely lad --
 The shadows dark'ning our intents -- Truth, sprung from heav'n --
 O stay! sweet is the least delay -- Welcome is the word.

743. Mason, George. The ayres that were sung and played at Brougham
Castle, 1618 (by) George Mason and John Earsden. Ed. by David Greer.
Menston, Eng.: Scolar Press, 1970. 24 p.

 Facsim. of the British Museum copy.

Series: English lute songs, v. 31.
Contents: SEE 742.

744. Greaves, Mason, Earsden: Songs (1604) and Ayres (1618). Trans.
and ed. by Ian Spink. London: Stainer & Bell; New York: Galaxy Music,
1963. 48 p.

Accomp. ed. from the lute tablature for keyboard instrument.
Series: ELS. Ser. 2, v. 18.
Contents: SEE 742.

JOHN MAYNARD

Literature

745. Dart, Thurston. "John Maynard." <u>Grove's dictionary of music and musicians, 5th ed</u>. New York: St. Martin's Press, 1954. V:639.

Brief mention of Maynard's volume of ayres.

746. Doughtie, Edward. <u>Lyrics from English airs, 1596-1622</u>. Cambridge, Mass.: Harvard University Press, 1970. 657 p.

747. Harwood, Ian. "John Maynard and 'The XII wonders of the world'." <u>LSJ</u> IV (1962):7-16.

748. Harwood, Ian. "Maynard, John." <u>The new Grove ...</u> London: Macmillan, 1980. XI:856-57.

749. Harwood, Ian. "Maynard, John." <u>MGG</u> VIII:1840-41.

750. Traficante, Frank. "Music for the lyra viol: the printed sources." <u>LSJ</u> VIII (1966):7-24.

751. Warlock, Peter. <u>The English ayre</u>. London: OUP, 1926. 142 p.

Reprint ed.: Westport, Conn.: Greenwood Press, 1970.
Chapter 10 is devoted to Maynard and others.

Music

752. Maynard, John. <u>The XII. wonders of the world. Set and composed for the violl de gambo, the lute, and the voyce to sing the verse, all three joyntly, and none severall: also lessons for the lute and</u>

base violl to play alone: with some lessons to play lyra-wayes alone,
or if you will, to fill up the parts, with another violl set lute-way
... Printed by Thomas Snodham for John Browne, and are to be solde at
his shop in Saint Dunstones Church-yard in Fleetstreete. 1611.

> RISM A/I/5 M1484.
> Contents: The courtier -- The divine -- The soldier -- The
> lawyer -- The physician -- The merchant -- The country gentle-
> man -- The batchelor -- The married man -- The wife -- The
> widow -- The maid.

753. Maynard, John. The XII wonders of the world, 1611. Ed. by
Ian Harwood. Menston, Eng.: Scolar Press, 1970. 52 p.

> Facsim. of the Bodleian Library copy.
> Series: English lute songs, v. 32.
> Contents: SEE 752.

Recordings

754. Maynard, John. The XII wonders of the world. Editions de
l'Oiseau-lyre DSLO 545, 1980.

> The Consort of Musicke; Anthony Rooley, conductor.
> Contents: SEE 752.

THOMAS MORLEY

Literature

755. Arkwright, G. E. P., H. C. Colles and Robert Donington. "Thomas Morley." Grove's dictionary of music and musicians, 5th ed. New York: St. Martin's Press, 1954. V:895-897.

Biography of Morley; includes a catalogue of his works.

756. Beck, Sydney. "The case of 'O mistress mine.'" RenaisN VI (1953):19-23.

757. Becker, Carl F. Die englischen Madrigalisten W. Byrd, T. Morley und John Dowland. Unpubl. Ph.D. diss., Bonn, 1901.

758. Brennecke, Ernest. "Shakespeare's musical collaboration with Morley." PMLA LIV (1939):139-49.

759. Brett, Philip. "Morley, Thomas." The new Grove ... London: Macmillan, 1980. XII:579-585.

Includes a list of Morley's works.

760. Brown, David. "Thomas Morley and the Catholics: some speculations." MMR LXXXIX (Mar./Apr. 1959):53-61.

761. Bush, H. E. "The recognition of chordal formation by early music theorists." MQ XXXII (1946):227ff.

762. Buttrey, J. "Music for Elizabeth I." Records and Recordings XIII/7 (1970:15.

763. Chibbelt, M. "Dedications in Morley's printed music." RMA Research XIII (1977):84-94.

764. Cutts, John P. "Seventeenth century songs and lyrics in Paris Conservatoire Ms. Res. 2489." MD XXIII (1969):117-39.

765. Dart, Thurston. "Discussion (of 'O mistress mine')" RenaisN VII (1954):15-17.

766. Dart, Thurston. "Morley and the Catholics: some further speculations." MMR LXXXIX (May/June 1959):89-92.

767. Dart, Thurston. "Morley's Consort lessons of 1599." PRMA LXXIV (1947/48):1-9.

768. Deutsch, Otto E. "The editions of Morley's 'Introduction.'" The library, 4th series, XXIII (1943):127-29.

      Notes differences between extant copies of early editions.

769. Doughtie, Edward. Lyrics from English airs, 1596-1622. Cambridge, Mass.: Harvard University Press, 1970. 657 p.

770. Doughtie, Edward. "Robert Southwell and Morley's 'First booke of ayres.'" LSJ IV (1962):28-30.

771. Duckles, Vincent. "New light on 'O mistress mine.'" RenaisN VII (1954):98-100.

772. Edwards, Warwick. The sources of Elizabethan consort music. Diss., University of Cambridge, 1974.

773. Flood, William H. "New light on late Tudor composers--XXIV. Thomas Morley." MT LXVIII (1927):228ff.

774. Gable, F. K. "Two songs in Shakespeare's 'Twelfth night'-- suggestions for practical performance." AmRec XIX (1978):52-56.

775. Gordon, Philip. "The Morley-Shakespeare myth." M&L XXVIII (1947):121-25.

776. Gray, W. "Some aspects of word treatment in the music of William Byrd." MQ LV (1969):45-46.

777. Greer, David. "The lute songs of Thomas Morley." LSJ VIII (1966):25-37.

778. Greer, David. "'What if a day'--an examination of the words and music." M&L XLIII (1962):304-19.

779. Harman, Richard. "Morley, Thomas." MGG IX:589-95.

780. Illing, R. "Barley's pocket edition of 'Est's metrical psalter.'" M&L XLIX (1968):219-23.

781. Joiner, Mary. "British Museum Add. Ms. 15117: a commentary, index and bibliography." RMA Research VII (1969):51-109.

782. Kerman, Joseph. "Morley and 'The triumphs of Oriana.'" M&L XXXIV (1953):185ff.

783. Mackerness, Eric David. The English musical sensibility; studies in representative literary discussions and periodical criticism from Thomas Morley (1557-1603?) to W. J. Turner (1899-1946). Ph.D. diss., Manchester (England), 1952.

784. McGrady, Richard J. "Thomas Morley's 'First booke of ayres.'" Music Review XXXIII (1974):171-76.

785. Monson, Craig A. Voices and viols in England, 1600-1650: the sources and the music. Diss., University of California, Berkeley, 1974.

786. Morley, Thomas. A plain and easy introduction to practical music. Ed. by E. H. Fellowes. Oxford: OUP, 1937.

    Facsim. ed.

787. Morley, Thomas. A plain and easy introduction to practical music. Ed. by Alec R. Harman. London: Dent, 1952. 326 p.

    This is a modernized annotated text with introduction by Thurston Dart. Includes facsimile and modern notation music examples.

788. Pattison, Bruce. "Notes on early music printing." The library, 4th ser. XIX (1939):389ff.

789. Pulver, Jeffrey. "The English theorists XIII--Thomas Morley." MT LXXVI (1935):411ff.

790. Ruff, Lillian M. "The social significance of the 17th century English music treatises." Consort XXVI (1970):412ff.

791. Seng, P. J. The vocal songs in the plays of Shakespeare. Cambridge, Mass.: Harvard University Press, 1967. 314 p.

    Includes a complete bibliography of Morley-Shakespeare literature.

792. Shaw, W. "Thomas Morley of Norwich." MT CVI (1965):669-73.

793. Smith, A. "The gentlemen and the children of the Chapel Royal of Elizabeth I: an annotated register." RMA Research V (1965):38-39.

794. Stevenson, R. "Thomas Morley's 'Plaine and easie introduction to the modes.'" MD VI (1953):177-84.

795. Warlock, Peter. The English ayre. London: OUP, 1926. 142 p.

    Reprint ed.: Westport, Conn.: Greenwood Press, 1970.
    Chapter 9 is devoted to Morley and others.

796. Wells, Robin H. "A setting of 'Astrophil and Stella' by Morley." EM VI (1978):230-31.

797. Wells, Robin H. "Thomas Morley's 'Fair in a morn.'" LSJ XVIII (1976):37-42.

798. Wienpahl, Robert W. "English theorists and evolving tonality."
M&L XXXVI (1955):378ff.

799. Zimmerman, Franklin B. "Italian and English traits in the music
of Thomas Morley." Anuario Musical XIV (1959):29-37.

Music

800. Morley, Thomas. The first book of ayres. Or little short songs,
to sing and play to the lute, with the base viole ... Imprinted at
London in litle S. Helen's by William Barley, the assigne of Thomas
Morley, and are to be sold at his house in Gracious Street. 1600.

>   RISM A/I/6 M3711.
>   Contents: A painted tale -- Thyrsis and Milla -- She straight
>   her light green silken coats -- With my love my life was nested
>   -- I saw my lady weeping -- It was a lover and his lass -- Who
>   is it that this dark night? -- Mistress mine well may you fare
>   -- Can I forget what reason's force -- Love winged my hopes --
>   What if my mistress now -- Come, sorrow, come -- Fair is a
>   morn -- Absence, hear thou my protestation -- Will you buy a
>   fine dog -- Sleep, slumb'ring eyes.

801. Morley, Thomas. The first booke of ayres, 1600. Ed. by David
Greer. Menston, Eng.: Scolar Press, 1977. 42 p.

>   Facsim. of the only known copy in the Folger Shakespeare Library,
>   Washington, D.C.
>   Series: English lute songs, v. 33.
>   Contents: SEE 800.

802. Morley, Thomas. The first booke of ayres (1600). Ed. by E.
Fellowes. London: Stainer & Bell, 1932. 40 p.

>   Original accomp. in lute tablature and modern notation.
>   Series: ESLS. Ser. 1, v. 16.
>   Contents: SEE 800.

803. Morley, Thomas. First book of airs, 1600. Ed. by E. H. Fellowes.
London: Stainer & Bell, 1952. 65 p.

>   Original accomp. is printed both in lute tablature and piano
>   Series: ELS. Ser. 1, v. 16.
>   Contents: SEE 800.

804. Morley, Thomas. First book of airs, 1600. London: Stainer &
Bell, 1959. 70 p.

>   For voice and piano; also includes original lute tablature.
>   Series: ELS. Ser. 1, v. 16.
>   Contents: SEE 800.

805. Morley, Thomas. <u>The first booke of ayres (1600)</u>. Rev. by
Thurston Dart. London: Stainer & Bell; New York: Galaxy Music, 1969.
40 p.

    Rev. ed.; lute accomp. printed in tablature and transcription.
    Series: ELS. Ser. 1, v. 16.
    Contents: SEE 800.

806. <u>An Elizabethan song book: lute songs, madrigals, and rounds</u>.
Music ed. by Noah Greenberg; text ed. by W. H. Auden and Chester
Kallman. New York: Doubleday, 1956.

    Contents: Mistress mine -- It was a lover and his lasse --
    Fair in a morne.

807. <u>Twenty songs from printed sources</u>. Trans. and ed. by David
Greer. London: Stainer & Bell, 1969.

    Series: ELS. Ser. 2, v. 21.
    Contents: O grief! e'en on the bud.

Recordings

808. Morley, Thomas. <u>The first booke of ayres (1600); to sing and
play to the lute, with base viole</u>. Telefunken 6.41127, 1970.

    Nigel Rogers, tenor; Nikolaus Harnoncourt, viola da gamba;
    Eugen M. Dombois, lute.
    Contents: SEE 800.

809. <u>Altenglische Lautenlieder</u>. Decca/Serenata 6.41648, 1960.

    Peter Pears, tenor; Julian Bream, lute.
    Also on container: Lute songs - Lautenlieder - Chansons au luth.
    Contents: Thyrsis and Milla -- I saw my lady weeping -- With
    my love, my life was nestled -- What if my mistress now.

810. <u>Elizabethan lute songs</u>. RCA Red Seal LSC 3131, 1970.

    Peter Pears, tenor; Julian Bream, lute.
    Contents: It was a lover and his lass -- Who is it?

811. <u>Elizabethan lute songs and solos</u>. Philips 6500 282, 1973.

    Frank Patterson, tenor; Robert Spencer, lute.
    Contents: Thyrsis and Milla -- Come, sorrow, come -- It was
    a lover and his lass.

812. <u>English lute songs and six In nomines</u>. Bach Guild BG-576, 1958.

    Alfred Deller, counter-tenor; Desmond Dupré, lute.
    Contents: Will ye buy a fine dog?

813. <u>An evening of Elizabethan verse and its music</u>. Columbia/
Odyssey 3216 0171, 1968.

    W. H. Auden; New York Pro Musica Antiqua; Noah Greenberg,
    director.
    Contents: I saw my lady weeping.

814. <u>History of music in sound. Vol. 4: The age of humanism. Solo
song</u>. RCA Red Seal LM 6029-2, 1954.

    Various performers.
    Contents: Thyrsis and Milla.

815. <u>Wandering in this place; witty, amourous and introspective ayres
and lute solos of Elizabethan England</u>. 1750 Arch 1757, 1977.

    Tom Buckner, voice; Joseph Bacon, lutenist.
    Contents: Can I forget what reason's force imprinted in my
    heart.

MARTIN PEERSON
(PEARSON)

Literature

816. Baxter, Robert M. <u>Martin Peerson's 'Mottects or grave chamber musique (1630)'</u> Unpubl. Ph.D. diss., Catholic University of America, 1970. 303 p. <u>Diss. Abst</u>. XXXI (Nov. 1970):2417a.

817. Eccles, M. "Jonson and the Spies." <u>Review of English studies</u> XIII (1937):392.

818. Emden, Cecil S. "Lives of Elizabethan song composers: some new facts." <u>Review of English studies</u> II (1926):416-22.

> Includes new biographical information on Ford, Pilkington, and Peerson.

819. Jones, Audrey M. <u>The life and works of Martin Peerson</u>. M. Litt., University of Cambridge, 1957.

820. Jones, Audrey M. "Martin Peerson: some new facts." <u>MMR</u> LXXXV (1955):172-77.

> Supplements: Wailes, M. "Martin Peerson."

821. Jones, Audrey. "Peerson (Pearson), Martin." <u>The new Grove ...</u> London: Macmillan, 1980. XIV:334-35.

822. Spink, Ian. "English seventeenth-century dialogues." <u>M&L</u> XXXVIII (1957):155ff.

823. Wailes, Marylin. "Martin Peerson." <u>Grove's dictionary of music and musicians, 5th ed</u>. New York: St. Martin's Press, 1954. VI: 612-14.

> Biography and catalogue of works.

824. Wailes, Marylin. "Martin Peerson." PRMA LXXX (1954):59-71.

Biographical with notes on music; reference to sources.

825. Wailes, Marylin. "Martin Peerson: 1571-1650." MMR LXXXII (1952):228-35.

826. Wailes, Marylin. "Some notes on Martin Peerson." Score IX (1954):18-23.

827. Warlock, Peter. The English ayre. London: OUP, 1926. 142 p.

Reprint ed.: Westport, Conn.: Greenwood Press, 1970.
Chapter 10 is devoted to Peerson and others.

Music

828. Peerson, Martin. Private musicke, or the first booke of ayres and dialogues, contayning songs of 4. 5. and 6. parts ... for voyces and viols, and for want of viols, they may be performed to either the virginall or lute. London: Thomas Snodham, 1620.

RISM A/I/6 P1135.
Contents: Open the door -- Resolved to love -- Ay, were she pitiful as she is fair -- Disdain that so doth fill me -- O precious time -- Can a maid that is well bred -- O I do love -- Since just disdain began to rise -- At her faire hands -- Now Robin laugh and sing -- Hey the horne -- Upon my lap -- Locke up faire lids -- Pretty wantons sweetly sing -- Sing, love is blind -- What need the morning rise -- Gaze not on youth -- The spring of joy is dry -- Is not that my fancy's queen -- See, O see who is here.

829. Peerson, Martin. "At her faire hands." For soprano solo and chorus (SATB) with keyboard. London: Schott, 1956. 3 p.

830. Peerson, Martin. "Disdain that so doth fill me." Trans. and ed. by Peter Warlock. London; Philadelphia: Curwen, 1926? 7 p.

831. Peerson, Martin. "Hey the horne." For soprano solo and chorus (SATB) with keyboard. London: Schott, 1956. 3 p.

832. Peerson, Martin. "Lock up, fair lids, the treasure of my heart." Trans. and ed. by Peter Warlock. London; Philadelphia: Curwen, 1926? 7 p.

833. Peerson, Martin. "Locke up faire lids." For soprano solo and chorus (SATB) with keyboard. London: Schott, 1953. 5 p.

834. Peerson, Martin. "Open the dore." For soprano (and/or tenor) solo and chorus (SATB) with keyboard. London: Schott, 1956. 3 p.

835. Peerson, Martin. "Resolve to love." For soprano solo and chorus (SATB) with keyboard. London: Schott, 1953.

836. Peerson, Martin. "See, I see, who is here (Seht, wer kommt hier)." For chorus (SSA with B ad lib) and keyboard. Mainz; London: Schott, 1959. 7 p.

837. Peerson, Martin. "Sing, love is blind." For soprano and alto soli, chorus (SAATB) with keyboard. London: Schott, 1953. 6 p.

838. Peerson, Martin. "Upon my lap." For soprano solo and chorus (SATB) with keyboard. London: Schott, 1953. 4 p.

839. English ayres, Elizabethan and Jacobean. Vol. I-VI. Trans. and ed. from the original ed. by Peter Warlock and Philip Wilson. London: OUP, 1927-31.

   Contents: Vol. IV. O precious time -- Now, Robin, laugh and sing -- O were she pitiful. Vol. VI. At her fair hands.

Recordings

840. Elizabethan love songs and harpsichord pieces. Lyrichord LLST 737, 1953.

   Hughes Cuenod, tenor; Claude Jean Chiasson, harpsichord. Contents: The falle of the leafe -- The primerose.

FRANCIS PILKINGTON

Literature

841. Brown, David. "Pilkington, Francis." The new Grove ... London: Macmillan, 1980. XIV:749-50.

842. Coxon, Carolyn. "Pilkington, Francis." MGG X:1276-77.

843. Doughtie, Edward. Lyrics from English airs, 1596-1622. Cambridge, Mass.: Harvard University Press, 1970. 657 p.

844. Emden, Cecil S. "Lives of Elizabethan song composers: some new facts." Review of English studies II (1926):416-22.

  Includes "new" biographical information on Ford, Pilkington and Peerson.

845. Fellowes, Edmund H. "Francis Pilkington." Grove's dictionary of music and musicians, 5th ed. New York: St. Martin's Press, 1954. VI:769-771.

  Biography with emphasis on Pilkington's madrigals, but his ayres are mentioned.

846. Newton, Richard. "The lute music of Francis Pilkington." LSJ I (1959):31-38.

847. Warlock, Peter. The English ayre. London: OUP, 1926. 142 p.

  Reprint ed.: Westport, Conn.: Greenwood Press, 1970. Chapter 9 is devoted to Pilkington and others.

Music

848. Pilkington, Francis. The first booke of songs or ayres of 4.
parts: with tableture for the lute or orpherian, with the violl de
gamba ... Printed by T. Estes, dwelling in Aldersgate-streete, and are
ther to be sould. 1605.

RISM A/I/6 P2370.
Contents: Now peep, Bo-peep -- My choice is made -- Can she
disdain -- Alas, fair face -- Wither so fast? -- Rest, sweet
nymphs -- Ay me, she frowns -- Now let her change -- Underneath
a cypress shade -- Sound, woeful plaints -- You that pine in
long desire -- Look, mistress mine -- Climb, O heart -- Thanks,
gentle moon -- I sigh, as sure to wear the fruit -- Down-a-down:
thus Phyllis sung -- Diaphenia, like the daff downdilly --
Beauty sat bathing by a stream -- Music, dear solace to my
thoughts -- With fragrant flowers -- Come, come all you.

849. Pilkington, Francis. The first booke of songs or ayres (1606).
Edited by David Greer. Menston, Eng.: Scolar Press, 1969. 53 p.

Facsim. of the British Museum copy.
Series: English lute songs, v. 34.
Contents: SEE 848.

850. Pilkington, Francis. The first book of songs or airs of four
parts: 1605. Ed. by G. E. P. Arkwright. London: J. Williams;
Oxford: J. Parker, 1897-98. 3 v.

For SATB, lute and piano reduction.
Series: The old English edition, no. 18-20.
Contents: SEE 848.

851. Pilkington, Francis. The first book of songs or airs of four
parts, 1605. New York: Kalmus, [19--]. 3 v.

Includes lute accomp. and accomp. arr. for piano.
Series: Kalmus vocal series, no. 6848-68.
Contents: SEE 848.

852. Pilkington, Francis. The first book of songs or airs, 1605.
Trans., scored and ed. from the original ed. by E. H. Fellowes. London:
Stainer & Bell, 1922-25. 2 v.

Series: ESLS. Ser. 1, v. 7, 15.
Contents: SEE 848.

853. Pilkington, Francis. The first booke of songs (1605). Ed. by
Edmund H. Fellowes; rev. by Thurston Dart; Assoc. reviser; David
Scott. London: Stainer & Bell; New York: Galaxy Music, 1971. 50 p.

Rev. ed.; original accomp. is printed both in lute tablature and
in modern notation.
Series: ELS. Ser. 1, v. 7, 15.
Contents: SEE 848.

854. Pilkington, Francis. <u>The first book of songs or airs of four parts</u>. Ed. by G. E. P. Arkwright. New York: Broude Bros., 1968. 3 v.

    Includes original lute accomp. and an arr. for piano.
    Series: The old English edition, v. 18-20.
    Contents: SEE 848.

855. <u>An Elizabethan song book: lute songs, madrigals and rounds</u>.
Music ed. by Noah Greenberg; text ed. by W. H. Auden and Chester
Kallman. New York: Doubleday, 1956.

    Contents: Now peep, boe peep -- Rest sweet nymphs.

856. <u>Forty Elizabethan songs</u>. Books I-IV. Ed. and arr. with original
accomp. by Edmund Horace Fellowes. London: Stainer & Bell, 1921-26.

    Contents: Rest sweet nymphs -- Diaphenia, like the daffdowndilly
    -- Down a down, thus Phyllis sung -- Now peek, boepeek.

                            Recordings

857. <u>Altenglische Lautenlieder</u>. Decca/Serenata 6.41648, 1960.

    Title on container: Lute songs - Lautenlieder - Chanson au luth.
    Peter Pears, tenor; Julian Bream, lute.
    Contents: Rest sweet nymphs.

858. <u>Ars Britannica: Old Hall Manuscript, madrigals, lute songs</u>.
Telefunken 6.35494, 1980.

    Pro Cantione Antiqua.
    Contents: Diaphenia -- Down-a-down.

859. <u>Choral music of Poulenc, Vaughan Williams, Holst, Byrd, Dowland</u>.
Lyrichord LLST 7177, 1966.

    Schola Cantorum of Oxford.
    Contents: Rest, sweet nymphs.

860. <u>Elizabethan love songs and harpsichord pieces</u>. Lyrichord LLST
737, 1953.

    Hughes Cuenod, tenor; Claude Jean Chiasson, harpsichord.
    Contents: Underneath a cypress tree.

861. <u>English ayres and duets sung in authentic Elizabethan pronunciation</u>.
Hyperion A66003, 1981.

    The Camerata of London.
    Contents: My choice is made.

862. <u>English lute songs and six In nomines</u>. Bach Guild BG-576, 1958.

Alfred Deller, countertenor; Desmond Dupré, lute.
Contents: Rest sweet nymphs.

863. <u>O ravishing delight; English songs of the 17th and 18th centuries</u>.
RCA Victrola VICS 1492, 1970.

Also released as: Harmonia Mundi DR 215, [197-]
Alfred Deller, counter-tenor; Desmond Dupré, lute and viola da
gamba.
Contents: Rest, sweet nymphs.

THOMAS ROBINSON

Literature

864. Austin, David L. <u>Thomas Robinson's 'The schoole of musicke.'</u> Unpubl. Master's thesis, University of Michigan, 1967.

865. Burleson, Richard F. <u>Thomas Robinson's 'Schoole of musicke':</u> <u>a lute tutor of 1603.</u> Unpubl. Master's thesis, University of Washington, 1967.

866. Dart, Thurston. "Thomas Robinson." <u>Grove's dictionary of music</u> <u>and musicians, 5th ed.</u> New York: St. Martin's Press, 1954. VII:193.

   Very brief biography of Robinson.

867. Frost, Maurice. <u>English & Scottish psalm & hymn tunes.</u> London: OUP, 1953. 531 p.

868. Greer, David. "'What if a day' -- an examination of the words and music." <u>M&L</u> XLIII (1962):304-19.

869. Harman, Richard. "Robinson, Thomas." <u>MGG</u> XI:584-85.

870. Harwood, Ian. "Thomas Robinson's 'General rules.'" <u>LSJ</u> XX (1978):78ff.

871. Kinkeldey, Otto. "Thomas Robinson's 'Schoole of musicke.'" <u>BAMS</u> I (1936):7ff.

872. Lumsden, David. "The schoole of musicke." <u>MT</u> CXIV (1973):493-94.

873. Poulton, Diana. "Robinson, Thomas." <u>The new Grove ...</u> London: Macmillan, 1980. XVI:76-77.

Music

874. Robinson, Thomas. The schoole of musicke: wherein is taught the
perfect method, of true fingering of the lute, pandora, orpharion, and
viol de gamba; with most infallible general rules, both easie and
delightfull. Also, a method, how you may be your owne instructor
for prick-song, by the help of your lute, without any other teacher:
with lessons of all sorts, for your further and better instruction.
London: Thomas Este, for Simon Waterson, 1603.

     RISM A/I/7 R1800.

875. Robinson, Thomas. The schoole of musicke (1603). Edition et
transcription par David Lumsden. Paris: CNRS, 1971. 75 p.

876. Twenty songs from printed sources. Trans. and ed. by David
Greer. London: Stainer & Bell, 1969.

     Series: ELS. Ser. 2, v. 21.
     Contents: Now Cupid, look about thee.

PHILIP ROSSETER

Literature

877. Fellowes, Edmund H. "Philip Rosseter." Grove's dictionary of music and musicians, 5th ed. New York: St. Martin's Press, 1954. VII:239-40.

   Discussion of Rosseter as a lutenist and composer.

878. Flood, William H. "New light on late Tudor composers -- XXX. Philip Rosseter." MT LXVIII (1927):1081ff.

879. Fortune, Nigel. "Philip Rosseter and his songs." LSJ VII (1965):7-14.

880. Fortune, Nigel. "Rosseter, Philip." MGG XI:930-32.

881. Greer, David. "'What if a day' -- an examination of the words and music." M&L XLIII (1962):304-19.

882. Harwood, Ian. "Rosseter's 'Lessons for consort' of 1609." LSJ VIII (1965):15-23.

883. Pattison, Bruce. "Philip Rosseter, poet and musician." MT LXXII (1931):986ff.

884. Poulton, Diana. "Rosseter, Philip." The new Grove ... London: Macmillan, 1980. XVI:211-12.

885. Vlam, Christian and Thurston Dart. "Rosseter in Holland." GalpinSJ XI (1958):63-69.

886. Warlock, Peter. The English ayre. London: OUP, 1926. 142 p.

      Reprint ed.: Westport, Conn.: Greenwood Press, 1970.
      Chapter 8 is devoted to Philip Rosseter.

Music

887. Rosseter, Philip. <u>A booke of ayres, set fourth to be song to
the lute, orpherian, and base violl</u> ... Printed by Peter Short, by the
assent of Thomas Morley. 1601.

RISM A/I/7 R2721.
Contents: Sweet come again -- And would you see my mistress'
face? -- No grave for woe -- If I urge my kind desires -- What
heart's content? -- Let him that will be free -- Reprove not
love -- And would you fain the reason know? -- When Laura smiles
-- Long have mine eyes gazed -- Though far from joy -- Shall I
come if I swim? -- Ay me, that love -- Shall then a traitorous
kiss? -- If I hope, I pine -- Unless there were consent -- If
she forsake me -- What is a day? -- Kind is unkindness -- What
then is love but mourning? -- Whether men do laugh or weep.

888. Rosseter, Philip. <u>A booke of ayres, 1601</u>. Ed. by David Greer.
Menston, Eng.: Scolar Press, 1970. 52 p.

Facsim. of the British Museum copy.
Series: English lute songs, v. 36.
Contents: SEE 887.

889. Rosseter, Philip. <u>Songs from Rosseter's Book of airs, 1601</u>.
London: Stainer & Bell, 1923. 2 v. (68 p.)

Two versions for each song: one with original lute accomp. in
tablature and in modern notation, and one with accomp. arr.
for piano. The part for the bass viol of the original ed. is
omitted.
Series: ESLS. Ser. 1, v. 8-9.
Contents: SEE 887.

890. Rosseter, Philip. <u>A book of ayres (1601)</u>. Ed. by Edmund H.
Fellowes; rev. by Thurston Dart. London: Stainer & Bell; New York:
Galaxy Music, 1966. 40 p.

Original accomp. is printed both in lute tablature and modern
notation.
Series: ELS. Ser. 1, v. 8-9.
Contents: SEE 887.

891. <u>An Elizabethan song book: lute songs, madrigals and rounds</u>.
Music ed. by Noah Greenberg; text ed. by W. H. Auden and Chester
Kallman. New York: Doubleday, 1956.

Contents: When Laura smiles.

892. <u>English ayres, Elizabethan and Jacobean</u>. Vol. I-VI. Trans. and
ed. from the original ed. by Peter Warlock and Philip Wilson. London:
OUP, 1927-31.

Contents: <u>Vol. I</u>. Though far from joy -- When Laura smiles --
Aye me, that love -- What then is love but mourning? <u>Vol. III</u>.

If she forsake me? -- Shall I come if I swim? <u>Vol. IV</u>. And would you see my mistress' face? -- What is a day? -- Whether men do laugh or weep. <u>Vol. V</u>. Kind is unkindness -- If I hope I pine -- Shall then a traitorous kiss?

893. <u>Forty Elizabethan songs</u>. Book I-IV. Ed. and arr. by Edmund Horace Fellowes. London: Stainer & Bell, 1921-26.

    Contents: <u>Book I</u>. When Laura smiles. <u>Book II</u>. If she forsake me. <u>Book III</u>. What then is love but mourning?

894. <u>The Oxford choral songs from the old masters</u>. London: OUP, 1923-29.

    Contents: And would you see my mistress' face -- What heart's content can he find? -- Let him that will be free -- What is a day? -- Whether men do laugh or weep.

895. <u>What is love?</u> Ed. and trans. by Carl Shavitz. London: Chester Music, [197-]

    Contents: What then is love but mourning?

Recordings

896. <u>Altenglische Lautenlieder</u>. Decca/Serenata 6.41648, 1980.

    Title on container: Lute songs - Lautenlieder -- Chansons au luth. Peter Pears, tenor; Julian Bream, lute. Contents: Sweet come again -- What is a day -- Whether men do laugh or weep.

897. <u>Elizabethan ayres and dances</u>. Saga 5470, 1980.

    James Bowman, countertenor; Robert Spencer, lute. Contents: Sweet, come again -- No grave for woe -- Shall I come if I swim -- What then is love but mourning -- Whether men do laugh or weep.

898. <u>Elizabethan love songs and harpsichord pieces</u>. Lyrichord LLST 737, 1953.

    Hughes Cuenod, tenor; Claude Jean Chiasson, harpsichord. Contents: When Laura smiles.

899. <u>Elizabethan lute songs</u>. RCA Red Seal LSC-3131, 1970.

    Peter Pears, tenor; Julian Bream, lute. Contents: If she forsake me -- What then is love but mourning -- When Laura smiles.

900. <u>Elizabethan lute songs and solos</u>. Philips 6500 282, 1973.

    Frank Patterson, tenor; Robert Spencer, lute.

Contents: Whether men do laugh or weep -- Sweet come again --
What then is love, but mourning.

901. English lute songs and six In nomines. Bach Guild BG 576, 1958.

Alfred Deller, countertenor; Desmond Dupré, lute.
Contents: When Laura smiles.

902. English songs of the 16th and 17th centuries. Abbey LPB 712,
1977.

Gerald English, tenor; David Lumsden, harpsichord/organ; Jane
Ryan, viola da gamba.
Contents: What then is love but mourning?

903. O ravishing delight: English songs of the 17th and 18th centuries.
RCA Victrola VICS 1492, 1970.

Also released as: Harmonia Mundi DR 215, [197-]
Alfred Deller, countertenor; Desmond Dupré, lute and viola da
gamba.
Contents: What then is love but mourning?

AUTHOR INDEX

TITLE INDEX

NOTE: Numbers in the Title Index refer to page numbers.

About the Compiler

Joan Swanekamp is head of Technical Processing at the Sibley Music Library of the Eastman School of Music, University of Rochester. She is the author of *Diamonds and Rust: A Bibliography and Discography on Joan Baez.*